MAKING SENSE OF THE CHILDREN ACT 1989

A Guide for the Social and Welfare Services
by
Nick Allen

Longman

Published by Longman Industry and Public Service
Management, Longman Group (UK) Ltd,
6th Floor, Westgate House, The High, Harlow, Essex
CM20 1YR
   Telephone: Harlow (0279) 442601
   Fax: Harlow (0279) 444501

British Library Cataloguing in Publication Data
Allen, Nick
   Making sense of the Children Act 1989: a guide for the
   social and welfare services.
   1. England. Children. Law
   I. Title
   344.202'87 ·

   ISBN 0-582-05742-6

ISBN 0-582-05742-6

Typeset by EMS Phototypesetting, Berwick upon Tweed
Printed and bound in Great Britain by
Biddles Ltd, Guildford and King's Lynn

Contents

Preface

The Children Act 1989 is a remarkable piece of legislation. Comprehensive in its scope and ambitious in its aims, it is destined to have a major impact on families in this country for many years to come. It will have a similar impact on those who work with children. This book is aimed firmly at non-lawyers. It is designed to provide suitably detailed guidance on the contents, and likely effects, of the Act. I am acutely conscious of the fact that different people hold different views on matters of child care law and policy and I have tried to maintain a balanced approach throughout.

Readers should note that, while most of the Act's provisions are not due to come into force until 1991, a few became effective at once. One of these amends the existing rules relating to access to children in compulsory care: unmarried fathers are now within the scope of these rules.

I should like to express my sincere thanks to Rod Jones of the Children's Division of Nottinghamshire County Council's Social Services Department, who kindly agreed to discuss with me various matters relating to the Children Act. My thanks also go to everyone at Longman who has helped in the production of this book (especially Alan Dearling) and to British Agencies for Adoption and Fostering for their support. Finally, I wish to mention the contributions made by my wife, Anne, and my children, Robert and Natalie. Their tolerance, support and encouragement have been tremendous.

Nick Allen
Nottingham Polytechnic Law School
December 1989

Acknowledgements

The publishers are indebted to the Controller of Her Majesty's Stationery Office for permission to reproduce extracts from DHSS *Review of Child Care Law* (1985); Butler-Sloss *Report of the Inquiry into Child Abuse in Cleveland 1987* (1988); House of Commons Social Services Committee *Children in Care* (1984); DHSS *The Law on Child Care and Family Services* (1987); Law Commission Working Paper No 96 (1986); Law Commission Supplement to Working Paper No 96 (1986); Law Commission Working Paper No 100 (1987); Law Commission Report No 172: *Guardianship and Custody* (1988); DHSS *Working Together* (1988); Department of Health *Protecting Children* (1988).

The publishers are also indebted to the London Borough of Greenwich for their permission to reproduce extracts from L. Blom-Cooper *A Child in Mind* (1987); Jane Rowe Caring Concern, *The Guardian* (June 2 1989).

1 Introduction

For many people working in the social services field, the advent of a new Children Act will occasion a feeling of despondency. The reaction will be: not another one, please! Such a reaction is entirely understandable, because if there is one outstanding feature of legal developments in the child care field in recent years it is the sheer bulk and frequency of legislation passed by Parliament, legislation which by virtue of its complexity has made this branch of the law virtually impenetrable to those without full legal training. Such a state of affairs is quite obviously unacceptable and the calls for reform have become louder and more numerous as time has gone by. The Children Act 1989 should be viewed as a response to this widespread dissatisfaction. It represents nothing less than a fresh start in this vitally important area of our law and for that reason alone it should be given a wholehearted welcome.

In this book I intend to look at the provisions of the new Act and consider their effects and implications, especially for those working in the social services. As we shall see, the Act not only tidies up the statute book − by bringing together numerous rules in a single coherent document − it also introduces many important changes in the substance of the rules themselves. It is, therefore, a reforming measure in every sense.

How many pieces of legislation concerning children have been enacted in the recent past? There is no single right answer to this question due to its lack of precision, but if we take 1969 as our starting point we can say without fear of contradiction that there have been at least 20 Acts of Parliament with a child law theme. I shall be taking a look at these Acts shortly, but before doing so I wish to bring into the discussion a couple of significant expressions.

Public and private child law

In the past few years, during the reform phase leading up to the Children Act, it has become fashionable to discuss the existing body of children's legislation by reference to two organising labels: public law and private law. These labels are quite important – if only because they are now used so much by government officials, other 'experts' and commentators – and so they deserve a mention here, but it is worth bearing in mind that they have no legal force. They do not appear in any legislation, for example, not even the Children Act itself. Nor have any official definitions been supplied. They are simply loose shorthand expressions which are used to describe different sets of statutory provisions. The names of the labels do in fact provide clues to their meaning.

'The public law relating to children' essentially means all the legislation concerning intervention in children's cases by public authorities. The work done by social services departments of local authorities obviously falls within this, but so does the work of voluntary organisations, even though these bodies are not statutory ones. The other label – 'the private law relating to children' – is really a residual one. It is taken to refer to the legislation which is primarily designed to deal with children's cases which, initially at any rate, do *not* involve public authorities. An example of this would be the Guardianship of Minors Act 1971 which, amongst other things, establishes a procedure for the judicial resolution of disputes between parents concerning the custody of their children. These two categories of public and private law are not completely self-contained – the Guardianship of Minors Act, for example, contains provisions enabling the court to commit the care of the child about whom the parents are in dispute to the local authority – but as a means of breaking up the legislation into reasonably distinct blocks for the purposes of discussion and debate, they have a useful role to play. Remember, however, that they have no legal force.

If we now take a look at the children's legislation passed by Parliament during the past 20 years and attempt to apply to it the public and private labels just described, we obtain the following result:

Public law

Children and Young Persons Act 1969
Children Act 1975
Child Care Act 1980
Foster Children Act 1980
Children's Homes Act 1982
Criminal Justice Act 1982
Health and Social Services and Social Security Adjudications
   Act 1983
Children and Young Persons (Amendment) Act 1986

Private law

Family Law Reform Act 1969
Guardianship of Minors Act 1971
Guardianship Act 1973
Matrimonial Causes Act 1973
Children Act 1975
Legitimacy Act 1976
Domestic Proceedings and Magistrates' Courts Act 1978
Child Abduction Act 1984
Child Abduction and Custody Act 1985
Family Law Act 1986
Family Law Reform Act 1987

Some of the Acts in this list are quite short. Others are very long. Taken together, they constitute a truly daunting body of law and of course there is also the pre-1969 material to consider. It is not just the bulk of the legislation which has caused problems, however. Many of the provisions have been drafted in a complicated fashion, many have been brought into force in dribs and drabs, and many have failed to produce an acceptable balance between the welfare of the child and the integrity of the family. These difficulties have been known about for a long time and the demands for a comprehensive revision of the law have become more and more insistent. Change was therefore inevitable. In the event, the impetuses for reform which were ultimately to prove crucial came from two separate sources outside government and it is at this stage that the significance of the public/private law distinction begins to emerge. The chronology is essentially as follows.

The 1984 report of the House of Commons Social Services Committee

This committee, made up of ten or so Members of Parliament, monitors the work of the Health and Social Security Departments and associated public bodies. In 1982 it decided to embark on an inquiry into children in care and accordingly took evidence from a large number of interested organisations. Its report was eventually delivered in 1984. This covered a great deal of ground and of its 108 recommendations, 26 were concerned with the courts, the law and entry into care. The central recommendation (for present purposes) speaks for itself:

> The time has arrived – indeed it arrived some time ago – for a thorough-going review of the body of statute law, regulations and judicial decisions relating to children, with a view to the production of a simplified and coherent body of law comprehensible not only to those

operating it but also to those affected by its operation. It is not just to make life easier for practitioners that the law must be sorted out; it is for the sake of justice that the legal framework of the child care system must be rationalised.

The 1985 Review of Child Care Law and the 1987 White Paper

The Department of Health, no doubt anticipating the Committee's proposal, acted quickly and a working party was established comprising officials from the relevant government departments together with representatives of the Law Commission, the standing law reform agency in this country. Discussion papers were circulated among interested organisations and in due course the working party's report was published under the title *Review of Child Care Law*. This 170 page document is important for all students of the Children Act, since it formed the basis of the Government's plans for reform of the 'public' part of child law, the official announcement of which came in January 1987 with the publication of the White Paper *The Law on Child Care and Family Services*. The White Paper stated that the Government's proposals would involve: 'a major overhaul of child care law intended to provide a clearer and fairer framework for the provision of child care services to families and for the protection of children at risk ... The Government will introduce legislation as soon as the Parliamentary timetable allows.' The Children Act is that legislation.

The Law Commission's review of private law

Alongside the examination of the public aspects of child law, there took place an in-depth review of the private law. This was undertaken by the Law Commission over the period 1984–1988 and involved the publication of four discussion papers followed by the issue of a report (*Review of Child Law: Guardianship and Custody*). In this report, the Law Commission observed that while the main principles of the existing law were reasonably clear and well accepted, the details were complicated, confusing and unclear. 'The result', it said, 'is undoubtedly unintelligible to ordinary people, including the families involved, and on occasions may prevent them or the courts from finding the best solution for their children.' By 1988, of course, the Government's plans for the public area had been announced. This meant that the Law Commission – which had itself played a significant part in the Review of Child Care Law – could frame its private law recommendations in such a way that the two areas would coalesce. Indeed, it went further, by annexing to its report a draft Bill designed to encapsulate both its own proposals and many of those contained in the Government's White Paper. The Children Act is based on this draft.

The Cleveland report

Looking at some of the statements which have been made during the passage of the Children Act, one would be forgiven for thinking that it represents a swift response by the Government to the recent events in Cleveland. The developments described above show that the Act is no such thing. The plain fact is that a comprehensive restatement of the law relating to children was clearly signalled, not only before the production of the Cleveland report in 1988, but also before the crisis itself occurred in the summer of 1987. By then, the DoH had published its White Paper on the reform of the public law, while the Law Commission's review of the private law was nearing completion. It is also worth remembering that the new legislation goes far beyond the areas of law dealt with in the Cleveland inquiry.

The Children Act is not, therefore, to be regarded as a response to Cleveland. Indeed, in some ways, the Cleveland affair has served only to distract attention in the reform process. That is not to say, however, that the events so carefully analysed in the Butler-Sloss report, and the report's own recommendations, are without significance. In the first place, the findings of the report have quite properly been used as a basis for discussing and testing the value of some of the Act's provisions. Secondly, one may reasonably expect certain aspects of professional practice to change in the light of the report's conclusions. I shall touch on both of these matters at appropriate stages in the book.

Implementation of the Act and the resources problem

It is the fate of nearly every piece of children's legislation that it is passed by Parliament with a sense of urgency but implemented by government in stages over a lengthy period. The Children Act 1989 may be no exception in this respect. Certainly there will be a delay in implementation – of up to two years, according to the Government – but whether there will be stages as opposed to introduction en bloc remains to be seen.

The Act is ominously silent on the question of resources. In the present climate it would be naïve in the extreme to expect local authorities and other agencies to be lavishly provided for in respect

of any of their functions. The fact remains, however, that expectations of the new legislation will be high and that these expectations
will only stand a chance of being satisfied if adequate funding is
made available for its operation.

   In view of the anticipated delay in implementation, I propose
throughout this book to use the expressions 'the existing legislation'
and 'the existing law' when referring to the statutory provisions and
judicial rulings which have effect at the time of writing.

Social work practice and agency policy

Will the Children Act greatly affect the way in which social workers
approach children's cases? It would be easy to give an unqualified
'yes' to this question – after all, this is a radical reforming statute on
any scale of measurement, and it covers a very wide range of
matters. Leading figures like Jane Rowe have already warned of the
'upheaval of professional thinking and practice' that it will require.
It is certainly true to say that the Act strengthens in a number of
ways the position of natural parents vis-a-vis social services
departments and highlights the need to preserve links between
children and their families. Having said this, though, it is still the
case that enormous discretion is given to social workers as regards
the way in which they discharge their responsibilities. If, for
example, we look at the provisions in the Act concerning preventative work, or child protection investigations, or applications for
compulsory powers, or parental and family contact, or the treatment
generally of children in care, we will find that the rules, and the
qualifications to the rules, are such as to give acres of room for
manoeuvre.

   Within this room, differences of emphasis will be able to flourish.
So that if, as has been argued (by Bob Holman in *Putting Families
First* (1988), Macmillan), child care social work has in the recent
past been split into two camps, the 'permanence school' and the
'preventative school', then this sort of divergence, and others, will
have little difficulty in surviving the Children Act. Social work
practices will certainly change under the Act but it would be foolish
to expect complete uniformity to emerge across the country.

Scotland and Northern Ireland

There are some provisions in the Children Act which apply to
Scotland and Northern Ireland, but not many. Furthermore, child
care law in Scotland is likely to be revised in the near future
following the establishment of a review body. Consequently, this
book is only concerned with the law of England and Wales.

2 Parental responsibility

Parental rights and duties

When the review of children's law began in earnest in 1984, it was realised that extended consideration would have to be given to the vexed question of parental rights and duties. It is indeed an obvious place to start, for what could be more fundamental in this particular context than the legal relationship between parent and child? In addition, how can the legal effects of court orders, and State intervention generally, be properly stated without some prior understanding of the nature of this relationship? Surely the one is founded on the other?

These are powerful arguments, and they would no doubt lead many people to anticipate a comprehensive statement (or restatement) of the parental rights and duties in the Children Act. But no such statement is there.

The existing law

Under existing law, there is no doubt that parents (by which I mean natural parents) have certain legal rights and duties in relation to their children. Indeed, some Acts of Parliament actually use the expression 'parental rights and duties' (e.g. the Children Act 1975). These rights and duties, however, are not set out in a single statutory document. Nor have the courts produced an authoritative catalogue; in fact, they have positively retreated from such an exercise. All that has happened is that legal commentators have scrutinised the various pieces of legislation concerning children, and have studied the different rulings of the courts over the years, and have come up with suggested lists of probable 'rights' and 'duties' which parents possess. They include the following:

Parental rights

1 The right to determine where the child should live.
2 The right to determine education.
3 The right to determine religion.
4 The right to discipline the child.
5 The right to consent to the child's marriage.
6 The right to authorise medical treatment.
7 The right to administer the child's property.
8 The right to appoint a guardian.
9 The right to agree to adoption.
10 The right to consent to a change in the child's name.

Parental duties

1 The duty to protect the child.
2 The duty to maintain the child.
3 The duty to secure the child's education.
4 The duty to control the child.

Several things need to be emphasised about this list. Firstly, it is unofficial in the sense that it is not directly derived from any single piece of legislation or court ruling. As previously stated, it is simply a list which can be said to be supported by a large number of different statutes and judicial decisions (e.g. the Marriage Act 1949 for the fifth right, the Adoption Act 1976 for the ninth right and the Education Act 1944 for the third duty).

Secondly, the expression 'parental rights and duties' is liable to mislead, because by no means all of the rights and duties in the list are exclusive to natural parents: some of them will in fact attach to anybody who happens to be caring for a child, irrespective of the existence of a biological tie. For example, there is no doubt that foster parents have both the right in law to discipline the child they are looking after and also the duty to protect him. This latter point was well illustrated by the widely publicised case which came before the High Court in May 1989 in which a woman sued her former foster parents for damages in respect of injuries suffered when she scalded her foot under a hot water tap. Although the claim failed on the facts, the judgement confirmed what has been acknowledged for many years, and that is that those caring for children must act as a reasonable parent would, taking the same degree of care to avoid foreseeable hazards.

Thirdly, the precise extent of some of these rights and duties is still in the process of being worked out. This is especially true of those rights and duties which flow, not from legislation, but from judicial rulings. Readers will no doubt recall the case brought a few years ago by Victoria Gillick against the Department of Health concerning the question of the provision of contraceptive advice and treatment to girls under the age of sixteen. Remarkably, that was the first occasion on which the English courts were directly faced with the task of explaining the so-called parental right to consent to medical treatment. The judges made some progress there but they also left a number of important questions hanging in the air. The answers will only come with further cases.

To summarise, then, the existing legislation certainly makes reference to the notion of parental rights and duties, as does the judicial case-law, but nowhere are these rights and duties clearly and authoritatively spelt out.

The effect of the new Act

The Children Act 1989 continues this tradition, although in an attempt to improve the legal framework it introduces an important new concept: 'parental responsibility'. One of the reasons why it is important is simply the frequency of its appearance in the Act. We will see, for example, that when a residence order is made by a court under section 8, the holder of the order is given parental responsibility. Similarly, when a care order is made under section 31, the local authority acquires parental responsibility. The Act also provides that natural parents will share parental responsibility in respect of their children, unless, that is, the parents are not married to each other, in which case the mother alone has it (although there are ways in which the father can acquire it).

What does this new concept mean? The Act defines it as follows:

> 'parental responsibility' means all the rights, duties, powers, responsibilities and authority which by law a parent of a child has in relation to the child and his property.

As can be seen, the concept is simply a shorthand term designed to cover the whole panoply of parental rights and duties. In this respect, it is similar, though not identical, to the existing statutory concept of 'legal custody' (which is what custodians acquire under the Children Act 1975). The 1989 Act is also similar to existing legislation in that it makes no attempt to define what the parental rights, duties, powers, etc. actually are. In the reform phase, the Law Commission took charge of this aspect of child law and it came to the view – correctly, it is suggested – that to attempt to produce an exhaustive and detailed list of the legal rights and duties of parents would be an unprofitable exercise. It felt that it would be a practical impossibility, as the list 'must change from time to time to meet differing needs and circumstances'. It might also be said that such an exercise would, without any doubt, prove to be exceedingly contentious, with no guarantee of public consensus at the end of the day. If evidence for this is needed, it is amply supplied not just by the Gillick case, but also by the controversy which developed during the passage of the Children Act concerning parents' and foster parents' 'rights' to inflict corporal punishment on their children.

'Parental rights and duties', therefore, continue under the new Act, but they are now subsumed under the all-embracing notion of parental responsibility. The introduction of the word 'responsibility' is essentially symbolic: it was felt by the Law Commission to reflect more closely 'the everyday reality of being a parent' and to be more in keeping with modern ideas relating to child care. The word 'rights', on the other hand, conjures up the idea of absolute power, which, as far as parent–child relationships are concerned, is not only outdated but also legally inaccurate, as the Gillick case itself demonstrated. The shift in emphasis from rights to responsibilities is therefore to be welcomed.

The initial allocation of parental responsibility

According to section 2 of the Act, where a child's father and mother were married to each other at the time of his birth, they shall each have parental responsibility for the child and each of them may act alone and without the other in meeting that responsibility. Whilst the statutory wording differs from the existing legislation, the substance is the same: married parents have had in law equal parental rights and duties for many years.

The Act enables either parent to take action in pursuance of their responsibility, without reference to the other. Joint decision-making by parents concerning their children's upbringing has obviously got a lot to recommend it but Parliament has wisely followed the Law Commission's proposal in not making it mandatory: it would be totally impractical. However, the Act is careful to make clear that this independence rule does not affect any statutory provision requiring both parents' consent (e.g. consent to adoption). Nor will a parent be able to act unilaterally if to do so would be incompatible with any court order which has been made (e.g. an order made following a divorce which requires one parent to consult the other before arranging holidays for the child). This last rule concerning court orders is one of the key provisions in the Children Act, as will be seen in later chapters of this book.

Unmarried fathers

For unmarried fathers, the rules are different. Here, parental
responsibility starts off with the mother exclusively. Again, however,
there is no real change in the law because unmarried fathers have
always been denied automatic and full recognition of their parenthood. While some – the present writer included – may have serious
misgivings about this, it would have been unrealistic to expect the
Children Act to do anything to alter the status quo. The reason why
this is so is that the traditional rule excluding fathers was reaffirmed
by Parliament as recently as 1987 when it passed the Family Law
Reform Act. That Act brought in many changes concerning children
born outside marriage, notably the abolition of affiliation proceedings, but it left intact the basic rule under discussion. The Law
Commission proposed no change and no change has been made.

Where, then, does this leave the unmarried father? The answer is
that the Children Act gives him the opportunity of acquiring
parental responsibility either by obtaining a court order or by
entering into a new-style written agreement with the mother. These
procedures are dealt with in the next section. In the absence of a
court order or an agreement, it might be thought that the father
would be completely bereft of any aspect of parental responsibility.
This is not the case, however. In the first place, he will always be
liable to maintain the child in the sense that the mother (and, given
the right circumstances, others) can apply to the court for an order
against him.

Secondly, if the father is actually caring for the child – and of
course very large numbers of them do this – from a legal point of
view he will be in a position to exercise the powers which any carer
has. These include powers in relation to education, religion,
discipline, medical treatment and change of name. At the same time,
he will have the duties to protect, educate and control the child. All
of this flows quite naturally from the characteristics of the 'rights'
and 'duties' mentioned, which depend for their existence not on any
blood tie or legal status but simply on the fact that the child is being
looked after by the person concerned. If the mother of the child is
opposed to the idea of the father possessing these powers, her
remedy is to remove the child from his care: the conventional
wisdom is that rights in relation to the child's place of residence rest
with the mother alone.

In this connection, however, it is suggested that account should be
taken of a new provision introduced by section 3 of the Children Act.
This states that a person who is caring for a child but who lacks
parental responsibility 'may do what is reasonable in all the
circumstances of the case for the purpose of safeguarding or
promoting the child's welfare'. This intriguing new rule – new in the

sense that it has not appeared in any legislation before – may be expected to generate a considerable number of questions. In the present context, it is likely that it could be relied upon by an unmarried father who is looking after his child so as to justify his refusal to allow the child's mother to resume caring for the child; the argument would be that the father reasonably thinks that the child would be at risk if he was released into the mother's care. Whether or not the Law Commission, which recommended the rule in section 3, intended it to have this effect is unclear (the only example of its significance which it gave concerned the making of arrangements by the child's carer for urgent medical treatment while his parents are on holiday) but the wording of the section certainly seems to permit it. Moreover, we shall see in a later part of this book that the provision has been interpreted in this fashion by the Government itself in relation to the legal position of foster parents.

Acquiring and losing parental responsibility

Married parents

As explained earlier, parents who are married to each other acquire parental responsibility automatically. They will not lose it until the child reaches the age of majority, unless the child is adopted or freed for adoption. If a court order other than adoption is made in respect of the child – an order following a divorce, for example, or a care order in favour of the local authority – others may well acquire parental responsibility but the parents will not lose theirs. This arrangement, whereby parental responsibility is enjoyed by several persons at the same time, reflects the Law Commission's view that the law should encourage parents 'to feel concerned and responsible for the welfare of their children' and that 'parents should not be deprived of their very parenthood unless and until the child is adopted'. However, it should be noted that there is applicable here the rule referred to earlier, that a parent may not act in any way which would be incompatible with a court order; so although parents will not lose parental responsibility when an order is made, their ability to exercise it will be restricted in accordance with the terms of the order.

Unmarried fathers

Unmarried fathers are, of course, in a special position, since automatic parental responsibility is denied them. One obvious way in which it can be acquired is through marriage to the child's mother. Another way is by making an application to the court (under section 4). If such an application is successful, parental responsibility will be shared. In this respect, the Children Act is no different from the existing law, since under the Family Law Reform Act 1987 the unmarried father may apply to the court for 'the parental rights and duties'.

The Law Commission noted, however, that court proceedings of this sort may be unduly elaborate, expensive and unnecessary. They therefore recommended a new procedure whereby mother and father could enter into an agreement which would have the same effect as a court order in favour of the father. This idea has now emerged in section 4 of the Children Act, which makes provision for 'parental responsibility agreements'. Whether these agreements will catch on with cohabiting couples is really anybody's guess, but there is little doubt that they are a more attractive proposition than going to a judge for an order.

The Act provides that a parental responsibility agreement must be made 'in the form prescribed' and recorded 'in the prescribed manner'. These prescriptions are not dealt with in the Act; they will be covered by government regulations, and the likelihood is that a standard official form will have to be completed and then checked at a court office. This aspect of the procedure is designed to emphasise its importance. It is also likely that the form will contain a statement in which the parents will be advised to seek legal advice if they are in any doubt as to the effect of entering into the agreement. The effect, of course, will be that the father, by acquiring parental responsibility, will gain access to the complete range of parental rights (and duties). Careful counselling of the parties will therefore be needed in some cases.

If the unmarried father does acquire parental responsibility, either through an agreement or a court order, it may be brought to an end by a later court order.

Third parties

Parental responsibility may be acquired by persons other than natural parents. This can happen through the making of a residence order under section 8 of the Children Act, a care order under section 31 and an emergency protection order under section 44. Adoption will also confer parental responsibility. These matters are covered in later chapters of this book. Another way, however, which will be dealt with here, is through the appointment of a guardian.

Under the existing legislation (primarily the Guardianship of Minors Act 1971), parents may appoint persons to act as guardians of their children after their death, but this must be done by deed or by will. Alternatively, the court may appoint a person to act as guardian where one or both parents have died. As the Law

Commission observed, very little is known about the practical operation of this legislation. The available statistics do not disclose the number of guardians, nor do they indicate the number of children who are potentially subject to guardianship. Furthermore, we have only limited knowledge of the sorts of circumstances in which guardians are appointed, the types of people who are actually appointed and the expectations of appointers and appointees. What research there is on the subject suggests considerable variation. In addition to this, the precise legal position of guardians, and the differences in law between guardians and parents, remain in many respects obscure.

Clearly, therefore, this is a subject ripe for revision and sections 5 and 6 of the Children Act are designed to restate the law so as to remove the existing uncertainties. They also introduce a number of changes in the substance of the rules. The main features of the new law are as follows:

- Guardians will have parental responsibility for the child. In other words, they will have access to the full range of the rights and powers described earlier, including the right to determine where the child is to live. They will also, of course, be subject to the usual parental duties.

- Parental appointments of guardians will no longer have to be made by deed or will. The new minimum requirement is that the appointment is in writing, is dated and is signed by the appointer or signed at his direction.

- A parental appointment will only take effect when the surviving parent dies. This represents a change to the existing law and has been introduced in an attempt to minimise the room for damaging conflict between the appointee and the surviving parent. The Law Commission put it this way:

  > Those, comparatively few, children who experience the death of a parent while they are under 18 will usually have been living with both parents at the time. There can be little doubt that those children's interests will generally lie in preserving the stability of their existing home and thus in confirming the continued responsibility of the survivor. There seems little reason why the survivor should share that responsibility with a guardian who almost invariably will not be sharing the household.

  As was pointed out, this rule will not prevent the surviving parent seeking guidance from the guardian, nor will it prevent the guardian taking action through legal proceedings (described in Chapter 4) if the situation requires it.

- The rule just described does not apply if the appointing parent held a residence order in respect of the child. In such a case, the appointment takes immediate effect on the death of the appointer. Residence orders, described in the next chapter, will replace custody orders under the existing legislation, and the situation envisaged here is that where the parents are living apart, perhaps divorced, with the caring parent having obtained this type of court order. The view which has prevailed is that if the caring parent dies having appointed a guardian for the child, the guardian should step into the picture immediately. This means that parental responsibility will be shared between the guardian and the surviving parent. Conflicts are obviously possible here, depending on the degree of involvement of the surviving parent, and if necessary court proceedings can be instituted in order to resolve them.

- The court may appoint a guardian either if the child has no parent or if one parent has died and that parent held a residence order in respect of the child. It can be seen that these conditions are very similar to those which apply to parental appointments.
- Parental appointments can be subsequently revoked.
- Persons appointed guardians by parents may disclaim their appointment within a reasonable time (regulations may lay down a procedure for doing this).
- A guardian may be removed at any time by court order.

These rules should do much to improve the law of guardianship. Their impact in practice, though, is impossible to predict. Certain kinds of case involving the death of a natural parent will continue to be better dealt with under the adoption law; others will require the intervention of the local authority or a voluntary organisation. Obviously many cases will continue to occur where no legal mechanism of any kind is necessary.

3 Court orders in favour of parents

Obscurity of the existing legislation

Consider the following not uncommon situations:

1   Husband and wife divorce. The court awards custody of their child to the wife.
2   Husband and wife divorce. The court makes a joint custody order in respect of their child.

What are the exact legal consequences of these court orders? Amazingly, we do not know the answer to this question, and the fact that we do not know is one of the many reasons why the Children Act is such a badly needed piece of legislation. One of the most fundamental objects of any 'private' children's law is to make clear the effect of orders of the court. In recent years it has been increasingly recognised that our existing legal framework is woefully deficient in this respect. The legislation is obscure on many vital issues and this obscurity has led to considerable speculation and, indeed, differences of opinion and practice among practitioners and judges.

This extraordinary state of affairs can be illustrated by reference to the first situation referred to above. This is concerned with orders for custody granted on or after a divorce. The statute in question, the Matrimonial Causes Act 1973, does not explain the meaning of the expression 'custody' – this, of course, is part of the problem – but the conventional view for many years was that a person granted custody in this way acquired a number of exclusive 'rights' over the child, covering not just his place of residence, but also such matters as his education, religious upbringing and medical treatment. In 1980, however, this general understanding was obliterated by a court ruling to the effect that a parent granted custody, far from being in a position of dominance, had a duty to consult the other about the future education of the child 'and any other major matters'. People working in the matrimonial field were completely unprepared for this ruling and, not surprisingly, the result has been utter confusion.

Complexity and inconsistency of the existing legislation

There are more than twelve separate statutory procedures authorising the courts to make orders for custody and access. In the words of the Law Commission, the provisions

> are neither clear nor consistent on such important matters as the meaning of custody, who may apply, which children are concerned, how their own point of view may be put before the court, what kinds of order may be made and what test the court should apply. The different powers are classic examples of ad hoc legislation designed for particular situations without full regard to how they fit into the wider picture.

Nobody could disagree with the Commission's conclusion that there is an unanswerable case for reform. The fact that each year some 170,000 children fall to be dealt with under the legislation obviously serves to reinforce this.

The new legal framework: Part II of the Children Act

Part II of the Children Act represents a new beginning as far as the private law is concerned. Its provisions will replace the following:

- The provisions concerning custody and access orders in divorce and other matrimonial proceedings.
- The provisions concerning custody and access disputes between parents (where no other issues are at stake).
- The custodianship law.
- The various provisions concerning access orders in favour of grandparents.

The principal objective is to set out in a clear and coherent manner a range of court orders and associated procedures which are necessary for the effective and sensitive disposal of private disputes and applications concerning the upbringing of children, whether such cases involve parents, relatives or 'strangers'. For reasons of convenience, I propose to deal separately with orders in favour of parents and orders in favour of non-parents. The present chapter is devoted to parents' cases.

Section 8 orders

The most obvious feature of the private law provisions of the Children Act is the appearance of four new types of court order. It is likely that these will be known collectively as 'section 8 orders' – indeed, the Act itself uses this terminology. These four orders, which are designed to supersede the various species of custody and access order to be found in the existing legislation, are:

1   The residence order
2   The contact order
3   The prohibited steps order
4   The specific issue order

These are the orders which the courts will use in future to settle issues between parents concerning children. The court will be able to make any, or all, of them, and it will be able to do this either in proceedings brought specifically for that purpose or in the course of other family proceedings where the central issue does not directly relate to children; a divorce case, for example, or an application for maintenance. We will see that the nature of the four orders is such that there is an infinite number of packages which the court can sanction at the end of the day. Given the enormous variety of situations which can arise in practice, this should be greatly advantageous.

Residence orders

According to section 8 of the Act, a residence order 'means an order settling the arrangements to be made as to the person with whom a child is to live'. Such an order would obviously be appropriate in a case where separating or divorcing parents were unable to reach agreement on the child's future home. It might also be suitable where an agreement has been reached by the parties but the circumstances suggest that a confirmatory order from the court would be beneficial.

Like the other section 8 orders, the residence order is designed to be flexible. The court could, if it wished, order that the child should live at all times with one parent. On the other hand, there is nothing to stop the court, where this is suitable, ordering the child's home to be divided between the two parents, with a precise timetable of moves being built in. The order can contain directions about how it is to be carried into effect and it can impose conditions which must be complied with by the parties. It can also be expressed to have effect only for a specified period or contain particular provisions which will only have a limited life. By using these supplementary powers imaginatively, the court should be in a position to tailor the residence order to the special requirements of the family concerned.

The position of the non-caring parent

The Law Commission, in framing its recommendations on the private law, was very anxious to do what it could to lower the stakes in matrimonial cases – to get away from the damaging 'winner takes all' approach which the existing custody legislation tends to generate. It wanted the law to emphasise instead the fact that parenthood continues even when marriage does not. The residence order is seen as playing a significant role here, because the Children Act is careful to make clear that the making of such an order will not destroy the parental responsibility which *both* parents possess. In principle, therefore, each party's rights and duties in relation to the child will be preserved.

A note of caution needs to be entered here, however. The Act also makes it clear that the fact that a person has parental responsibility 'shall not entitle him to act in any way which would be incompatible with any order made with respect to the child'. So if a residence order is made in favour of, say, a wife, her husband will certainly retain his parental responsibility for the child, but he will have to make sure that in exercising it he does not interfere with the arrangements set out in the order, otherwise he will be in contempt of court. His power to remove the child will consequently be curtailed (unless, that is, the wife agrees to the removal, for a person who holds a residence order will be quite free to arrange for someone else to care for the child). This does obviously mean that the scope for actually making use of parental responsibility in a case where the other parent has been granted a residence order may in practice be rather limited. Choice of school, for example, is a matter which largely goes hand in hand with residence.

Having said this, the legal position is not entirely one-sided. In the first place, one of the other section 8 orders (see below) may be made along with the residence order, which may well have the effect of enhancing the position of the non-caring parent. A similar result will often be achieved by attaching special conditions to the residence order. Secondly, the Children Act itself contains provisions designed to prevent unilateral action in relation to two specific matters: the removal of the child from the UK and the changing of the child's surname. Where a residence order is in force, nobody may take such action without either the written consent of every person who has parental responsibility or the leave of the court (which would obviously aim to act in the child's best interests). These rules, which are modelled on parts of the existing legislation, have been deemed necessary in view of the particularly serious nature of the acts in question. There is an exception to the prohibition on removal from the UK, and that arises where the holder of the residence order takes the child abroad for less than one month, but this is subject to any special conditions (e.g. regarding notice to the other parent or the maximum number of journeys abroad that can be made) that the court may choose to impose. Thirdly, the law relating to adoption will continue to insist on the consent of both parents being obtained (subject to dispensing by the court) before such an order is made.

Contact orders

A contact order means 'an order requiring the person with whom a child lives, or is to live, to allow the child to visit or stay with the person named in the order, or for that person and the child otherwise to have contact with each other'. This is the new form of access order.

As with the other section 8 orders, special directions and conditions can be built into the contact order, and no doubt there will continue to be great variety in the sort of provision which is made by the courts; and, like residence orders, one can expect contact orders to be made in very large numbers.

If a contact order is made in favour of a parent, he will be able to exercise parental powers during the period of contact. Care will have to be taken, however, not to go too far, because he will be subject to the rule that a person with parental responsibility may not act in any way which would be incompatible with any court order. So if special conditions have been incorporated into the contact order, or if a residence order has been made in favour of the other parent, he will have to ensure that he conducts himself consistently with them. The Law Commission illustrated the point in this way:

> If the child has to live with one parent and go to a school near home, it would be incompatible with that order for the other parent to arrange for him to have his hair done in a way which will exclude him from the school. It would not, however, be incompatible for that parent to take him to a particular sporting occasion over the weekend, no matter how much the parent with whom the child lived might disapprove.

Prohibited steps orders

These orders are designed to deal with potential trouble spots in family relationships. They will enable the court to order that 'no step which could be taken by a parent in meeting his parental responsibility for a child, and which is of a kind specified in the order, shall be taken without the consent of the court'.

Such orders could well be useful in cases where the court felt that it ought, in the child's interests, to have some sort of supervisory role in relation to some important aspect of his upbringing. An example might be the question of medical treatment, or moving to a distant part of the country (or abroad), or changing schools. Questions such as these have the capacity to generate prolonged and acrimonious arguments between estranged parents, and if in any particular case they seem likely to arise, with little prospect of agreement, the court might feel that the best solution would be for it to retain a hold on the matter.

Needless to say, the making of a prohibited steps order will reduce – perhaps considerably, depending on what is in the order – the freedom possessed by the parent who is caring for the child, and this could easily undermine that parent's confidence and sense of security, which in turn could be damaging for the child. Great care will therefore be needed in judging whether or not this particular part of the Act should be activated. The Law Commission thought that orders of this kind would be 'few and far between'.

Specific issue orders

A specific issue order is an order 'giving directions for the purpose of determining a specific question which has arisen, or which may arise, in connection with any aspect of parental responsibility for a child'.

Such an order can be used to settle, in what the court sees as the best interests of the child, a single issue which has sprung up between the parents and on which they are unable to agree, e.g. whether or not their child should attend church, or have his ears pierced, or participate in a hazardous sport – the possibilities are endless.

The order can also be used, however, to settle an issue in advance of its arising. An example of this would be where the court grants a divorce and makes a residence order in favour of the wife, who is a Jehovah's Witness, but goes on to make a specific issue order under which the child is not to be deprived of a blood transfusion by the wife should such an operation ever be deemed necessary. In these circumstances, the wife would be obliged to act in accordance with the court's direction if the situation in question occurred.

The criterion for section 8 orders

So far, we have looked at the new range of private orders which the
Children Act enables the court to make. On what basis ought the
court to act when the question of making an order arises? On this,
the Act makes no great change in the existing law, for its opening
provision (section 1(1)) reads:

> When a court determines any question with respect to the upbringing of
> a child, the child's welfare shall be the court's paramount consideration.

This welfare principle has been a feature of our private law
legislation since 1925 and, in spite of the criticisms levelled at it (too
vague, unpredictable and value-laden in its application, productive
of inconsistencies) it has proved to be the best available criterion in
the sort of cases at which it is aimed. It has therefore been retained.
In the existing legislation, the principle is to be found in section 1 of
the Guardianship of Minors Act 1971, where the words 'first and
paramount consideration' are used. As can be seen, the word 'first'
has been dropped from the statutory formula. This has been done on
the grounds that, firstly, it is superfluous, and secondly, it could lead
the reader to believe that considerations other than the child's
welfare (e.g. doing 'justice' to one parent) are of equal weight in the
decision-making process.

The Children Act goes on to supplement the welfare principle
with four further provisions. The first, section 1(3), contains a
checklist of factors for the court to bear in mind in any disputed case.
This checklist is not particularly novel, in that it is modelled on
existing good practice, but its prominent presence in the legislation
will do no harm and may even prevent some unsuitable decisions
being made. It should also facilitate the preparation of cases. The
factors in this list are as follows:

(a) the ascertainable wishes and feelings of the child concerned
     (considered in the light of his age and understanding);
(b) his physical, emotional and educational needs;
(c) the likely effect on him of any change in his circumstances;
(d) his age, sex, background and any characteristics of his
     which the court considers relevant;
(e) any harm which he has suffered or is at risk of suffering;
(f) how capable each of his parents, and any other person in
     relation to whom the court considers the question to be
     relevant, is of meeting his needs;
(g) the range of powers available to the court under the Act in
     the proceedings in question.

Care needs to be taken with this checklist. In the first place, it is not exhaustive; other factors will in some cases be relevant. Secondly, the arrangement of the factors in lettered paragraphs (a) to (g) is not meant to imply an order of descending importance, it is simply the draftsman's way of setting them out in a readable fashion. As has been the case for many years now, there are no 'rules' for deciding the outcome of children's cases; each case is unique and should be judged on its own particular facts. Having said this, however, it is certainly no accident that the wishes and feelings of the child have been put at the forefront of the checklist. This, as with many other parts of the Children Act, symbolises the unmistakeable trend in recent years towards giving proper weight to the child's voice. But that voice is not automatically conclusive, even if it belongs to a teenager – at the end of the day, how much weight is 'proper' must depend on the facts.

To comply with its duty to have regard to all the matters contained in the checklist and to any other circumstances relevant to the child's welfare, the court will obviously require a considerable amount of information. Much of this will come via social workers' reports, a matter discussed in Chapter 14 of this book.

The second supplementary provision, section 1(5), is equally important. It reads:

> Where a court is considering whether or not to make one or more orders under this Act with respect to a child, it shall not make the order or any of the orders unless it considers that doing so would be better for the child than making no order at all

The wording of this subsection makes it clear that it covers all orders under the Act, i.e. public law ones as well as private; consequently, it will become relevant – very relevant, in fact – in the discussion of care orders etc. later on. For the moment, however, we need to consider its significance in the context of parents' cases.

Where estranged parents are in serious dispute about some aspect of their child's upbringing and an application to resolve the matter is made to the court, then an order of some sort will probably be needed. It will have a positive function. Where estranged parents are involved in legal proceedings for divorce or maintenance, but there is no dispute regarding their child's upbringing, should any children's order be made? This is the issue addressed by section 1(5). Research carried out for the Law Commission revealed that many lawyers who represent wives in matrimonial proceedings tag an application for custody onto the claim, even if there is no likelihood of a dispute over the children arising: 'a custody order is "part of the package" for the client and will be requested from the court as a matter of course'. It is clear that many judges and magistrates have been sucked into this mechanical approach as well.

If no section 8 order is made on, say, a divorce, then quite obviously the existing legal position with regard to the parents' powers and duties will continue, so that they will each retain the independent power to act. In many cases, there is absolutely no reason why this should not be so. It goes without saying that children's orders can have beneficial effects even in the absence of a dispute – the reinforcement of a new family unit, for example – but they also contain a significant potential to be used as psychological weapons or viewed as the winner's prize, thereby reducing the prospects of co-operation between the parents in the future. The inclusion of section 1(5) is therefore an important reminder that court orders should not be regarded as in any way routine but should be made only where they are likely to bring about real benefits for the child concerned.

The other supplementary provisions, concerning delays, are discussed in the next section.

Countering delays in legal proceedings

The problems associated with delays in children's cases are too obvious to need rehearsing here. One of the innovations contained in the Children Act is the collection of provisions designed to prevent them. For private law cases, there are two main provisions, set out in sections 1 and 11. One provision is general, the other is specific.

The general provision requires the court to have regard to the principle that any delay in determining a question concerning a section 8 order is likely to prejudice the welfare of the child involved. This is a reminder both for the courts and for practitioners to give priority to children's cases wherever possible. It is to be hoped that it will also serve as a reminder to governments that adequate resources are vital for the proper management of such cases.

The specific provision requires the court to draw up a timetable in every case 'with a view to determining the question without delay'. Directions may be given to the parties so as to ensure that the timetable is adhered to. If the Act stopped there, the features of each timetable would be left to the unfettered and unguided discretion of the court; in an effort to introduce some consistency, however, section 11 enables supplementary 'rules of court' – in effect, government regulations – to be made. These rules are likely to be quite detailed and may well specify optimum timescales for particular types of case. No doubt the question of extensions will be covered as well.

Whilst delays in family litigation can be damaging to all the adults and children involved, it is a well-known fact that the dragging-out of a case can be, and is, used as a weapon in itself, especially by a party who currently has the care of the child and who is aware of the reluctance of the courts to disturb established arrangements. What can be done to prevent such manoeuvres? This is an extremely difficult question. In the final analysis, if the court has set a timetable which one party has for no good reason disregarded, penalties for contempt of court can be imposed. No mention is made of these penalties in the Act, perhaps for reasons of tact, but there is no doubt that they will be available in suitably extreme cases. Their very existence should therefore have some deterrent effect. As is so often the case with contempt of court applications, however, punishing the offender can have the effect of punishing the child as well. The fact is that the law can only offer so much by way of assistance in this delicate field.

Family assistance orders

Section 16 of the Children Act introduces another new type of order: the family assistance order. Such an order can be made in any family proceedings, whether or not any other type of order is made. A large proportion of them are likely to be made in divorce proceedings.

The present position is that in divorce, maintenance, custody and adoption cases the court may, in exceptional circumstances, make an order that the child 'be under the supervision' of a probation officer or a local authority. These matrimonial supervision orders, as they are often called, are quite distinct from supervision orders made by the juvenile court in care proceedings under the Children and Young Persons Act 1969, but of course they share the same name, and experience has shown that there is considerable confusion and variation regarding their making, implementation and general significance. The opportunity has therefore been taken of revising both the wording and the substance of the rules.

The main features of section 16 are as follows:

- The family assistance order will impose a duty on the probation service or the local authority to make an officer available to advise, assist and (where appropriate) befriend any person named in the order.
- The persons who can be named in the order are the child, his parents or guardian and any other person who is caring for him or who holds a contact order with respect to him.
- The order may only be made in exceptional circumstances.
- The consent of every person named in the order (other than the child) must be obtained.
- Any person named in the order can be required to keep the assisting officer informed of relevant addresses so as to facilitate visits.

- The order is to last for no more than six months.
- The assisting officer may return to court at any time and ask it to consider varying or discharging any section 8 order it has made.

It will be apparent that the family assistance order provisions are aimed at situations where it is felt that short-term social work support would be welcomed by the parties and would be beneficial for the child concerned. It is a voluntary procedure and is certainly not to be looked upon as part of the machinery of compulsory State intervention – that is governed by the completely separate set of provisions in the Act relating to care orders, supervision orders, emergency protection orders etc. If, in a divorce or other family case, it is thought that the child is at risk, then those other provisions may be activated, assuming of course that the relevant statutory grounds can be made out.

As with existing matrimonial supervision orders, these new-style assistance orders will have a part to play in a wide variety of circumstances (for example, the facilitation of contact arrangements, enabling advice and support to be given to a new family unit, providing mediation between the parties) but of course the Act continues to require those circumstances to be 'exceptional'. This criterion is obviously vulnerable to criticism on account of its vagueness, but its retention was advocated by the Law Commission on the grounds that it 'may be at least partially effective in concentrating resources where they are most needed'. The resources in question will be those of either the probation service or the local authority; which agency is selected will depend, as at present, on the circumstances of the case and on any local arrangements which have been established. In many cases, the social worker providing the welfare report for the court will be appointed as advisor. It is likely that the courts will be asked, as a matter of practice, to make it clear to the social worker in each case why family assistance has been ordered.

Unmarried fathers and section 8 orders

It was seen in the last chapter how the Children Act preserves the existing principle that the parental rights and duties in respect of a child born outside marriage vest initially in the mother alone. It was also seen how the Act enables the father to acquire 'parental responsibility' through an application to the court or through an agreement made with the mother. Whether or not such acquisition has taken place, the four types of section 8 order described in this chapter can all be sought by the unmarried father against the mother. If any such order is made, her powers will be restricted accordingly, for she will be unable to act in any way which is incompatible with it.

In this connection, it is worth noting that should the father succeed in obtaining a residence order from the court, and he has not previously acquired parental responsibility, the Act requires the court to make in addition an order giving that responsibility to him. This will enable him to exercise the full range of 'rights' recognised by law. The Law Commission felt that it would be wrong to deny these to a father who was going to have the child living with him. Remember, though, that even if this does take place, the court may decide to build conditions into the residence order and/or make another section 8 order in favour of the mother.

Other aspects of section 8 orders

There are a number of other provisions in the Children Act which are relevant to the theme of this chapter and which deserve a mention. They are listed below.

- A section 8 order cannot be made with respect to a child who has reached the age of sixteen unless the circumstances are exceptional. This rule is a further illustration of the increasing recognition being given to the autonomy of the older child.
- A section 8 order will cease to have effect when the child reaches the age of sixteen (unless the court orders otherwise).
- All section 8 orders may be varied or discharged by the court.
- In relation to divorce cases the much-criticised existing provisions, under which the court must declare itself satisfied with the arrangements made for the children before it terminates the marriage, are replaced by a new rule which simply requires the court to consider whether it should exercise any of its powers under the Children Act.
- Residence orders and contact orders made in favour of one parent will automatically come to an end if the parents live together for more than six months. For the orders to continue in these circumstances would be unrealistic.
- Section 8 orders are automatically discharged if a care order is made in respect of the child.
- On disposing of a section 8 application, the court may order that no further applications are to be made except with its permission ('we have in mind the sort of case where, after a fully argued hearing, a parent is denied contact, or granted only carefully defined contact, with the child but seeks a further order shortly afterwards. Vindictive or obsessive harassment of this kind is regrettably not unknown and it can

seriously undermine the security and happiness of the child's home': the Law Commission).

- No section 8 order, other than a residence order, may be made in respect of a child who is the subject of a care order. This matter is discussed in Chapter 10 but it may be noted here that parents who wish to obtain a court order concerning contact with their child in care can use the procedure laid down in Part IV of the Act.

- Although the existing legislation concerning custody orders is repealed by the Children Act, the provisions of the Child Abduction Act 1984 and the Family Law Act 1986 are retained. The 1984 Act imposes criminal liability for certain abductions, while the 1986 Act contains provisions relating to the enforcement of orders (for example, it gives the court power to order a person to disclose the child's whereabouts). The 1989 Act amends these two earlier Acts so that they now refer to the new types of court order.

4 Court orders in favour of non-parents

The scope of the present chapter

The last chapter was concerned with children's cases brought by, and only involving, natural parents. This chapter aims to cover other private law applications. In view of their diversity, it may be useful to summarise at the outset the main types of situation falling under this heading and the way in which the existing law makes provision for them.

1 Applications by step-parents

A step-parent may apply for custody or access if he or she is involved in divorce proceedings (under the Matrimonial Causes Act 1973) or in maintenance proceedings (under the Domestic Proceedings and Magistrates' Courts Act 1978), provided the child concerned is a 'child of the family', i.e. has been treated by husband and wife as a child of their family. Step-parents may also, in some circumstances, apply for custodianship under the Children Act 1975, or for custody under the Matrimonial Causes Act where they marry a divorced natural parent. Obtaining a custodianship or custody order will provide legal recognition of their position as carer of the child.

2 Applications by relatives

The only relatives singled out by the existing private law legislation are grandparents. Provisions dating from 1978 enable the court to make an access order in favour of a grandparent in a number of family proceedings. Apart from this, relatives generally may apply (subject to certain conditions) for a custodianship order. It is also possible for relatives to apply for custody in the context of a divorce case.

3 Applications by foster parents

In certain circumstances, foster parents may apply for custodianship.

In addition to these statutory procedures, it is open to a step-parent, relative or foster parent (or, for that matter, any interested person) to institute wardship proceedings in the High Court with a view to obtaining an order relating to the upbringing of the child. Nor should it be forgotten that in appropriate cases the adoption jurisdiction is available for use as well, and that the legislation enables the court to refuse an adoption order but grant custodianship instead.

The creation of this network of provisions was undoubtedly well intentioned. As with the law relating to parental applications, however, it is neither simple nor clear nor consistent. This is true even of the custodianship rules, which only came into operation in 1985 and were supposedly tailor-made for non-parents. The Children Act enables a fresh start to be made.

Section 8 orders in favour of non-parents

We saw in the last chapter how section 8 of the Children Act has been designed to improve the private law by introducing four new types of court order: residence orders, contact orders, prohibited steps orders and specific issue orders. The important point for the purposes of this chapter is that these orders will generally speaking be available to non-parents, as well as parents, and available in cases specially brought for the purpose or in cases where some other family issue is at stake (e.g. divorce). They will supersede the existing orders for access, custody, and custodianship. Wardship and adoption will remain available, but the need to resort to wardship should be diminished by the creation of these new orders (this matter is explored in Chapter 15).

The nature of these four orders has already been described, and it is not proposed to repeat the descriptions here. Suffice it to say that their availability, coupled with the fact that specially crafted conditions can be incorporated into them by the court, will mean that a position of great flexibility is achieved. The effect of the court's order should also be clearer than it is under the present arrangements. Here are some examples of what could be done under the new regime:

- The court makes a residence order in favour of a foster parent. This will enable the foster parent to keep the child, even if the natural parents and the local authority object.
- The court makes a contact order in favour of the child's aunt and uncle. The person caring for the child will have to permit the child to visit, and perhaps stay with, these relatives.
- The court makes a prohibited steps order in favour of the child's grandparent: the order prohibits the child's parents from removing the child from his present school without the court's consent.
- The child's parents have arranged for him to undergo an operation: relatives obtain a specific issue order preventing the operation going ahead.

Needless to say, all cases brought under section 8 will be subject to the principle that the child's welfare is to be the paramount consideration. The wishes and feelings of the child, and all the other matters referred to in the statutory checklist (in section 1), will have to be taken into account, at any rate if the case is contested. Also applicable will be the rule under which the court is not to make an order unless it considers that doing so would be better for the child than making no order at all.

Special rules for non-parents' applications

Court applications by non-parents, especially relatives and 'strangers', tend to contain special features and consequently throw up special problems. The risk of the application being an unwarranted intrusion into the child's life is one which obviously springs to mind. The Children Act contains provisions designed to impose a proper balance between the various interests which can exist in these cases.

The need to obtain leave

First of all, non-parents will as a rule have to obtain leave from the court to make an application for a section 8 order. This, clearly, is directed at the intrusion point. The argument is that without some sort of preliminary procedural hurdle, the way would be open for the bringing of all sorts of unnecessary and unmeritorious legal proceedings, the effect of which could be extremely damaging for the child concerned. This is, in fact, brought out fairly explicitly in the Children Act, for it states (in section 10) that in deciding whether or not to grant leave, the court shall have particular regard to the following:

(a)   the nature of the proposed application;
(b)   the applicant's connection with the child;
(c)   any risk there might be of the application disrupting the child's life to such an extent that he would be harmed by it;
(d)   where the child is being looked after by a local authority, the authority's plans for the child's future and the wishes and feelings of the child's parents.

As a result of the above-mentioned provisions, we may expect the courts to scrutinise non-parental applications with particular care. Having said this, there are bound to be cases where the facts are such that the obtaining of leave is more or less a formality. As always, there are no rigid rules, except that the child's welfare is paramount; everything depends on the circumstances.

The special position of children in care

Paragraph (d) above is obviously directed at applications concerning children in care, whether they are in care as a result of a care order or as a result of voluntary arrangements made with the family. It is one of a number of provisions in the Act which are designed to deal with the difficult problem of providing easy access to the courts for foster parents and relatives where an order in their favour would benefit the child, while at the same time promoting confidence in the public child care system among natural parents and allowing local authorities the necessary measure of freedom to plan ahead. The response of the Act, as far as section 8 applications by foster parents and other non-parents are concerned, is essentially two-fold.

Firstly, foster parents (and persons who have been foster parents within the last six months) who have had the child for less than three years will need the consent, not only of the court, but also of the local authority, if they are to make an application for a section 8 order (and we are really talking about residence orders here). The only exception to this rule covers foster parents who are relatives. The rule, contained in section 9(3), quite clearly puts the local authority firmly in the driving seat in the situation described. The statutory dividing line of three years is fairly arbitrary, of course, but it appears in the present custodianship law and has been defended by the Government on the grounds that a shorter period would carry with it too many dangers. As will be seen shortly, foster parents who have cared for the child for *more* than three years are not subject to any leave requirement at all as far as residence and contact orders are concerned.

The second response of the Act is paragraph (d) of section 10(9), set out above. This requires the court to have regard to the local authority's plans and the views of the natural parents when deciding whether or not to grant leave to apply for a section 8 order. A relative wishing to apply for a residence order in respect of a child in care would be caught by this provision. It is not, however, as onerous as the rule governing the foster parent with less than three years care, since it does not give the local authority a power of veto – it simply directs the court to consider the authority's intentions.

Non-parents who do not need leave

Not every non-parent will be subject to the leave requirement. In certain circumstances, the requirement is felt to be unnecessary:

- A person who has already been granted a residence order has the right to apply for any section 8 order in the future. So, for example, a foster parent holding a residence order could apply, without leave, for a specific issue order if a dispute arose with the natural parents over the child's schooling. As a residence order will confer 'parental responsibility' on the holder, access to the court should be unfettered.
- A husband or wife has the right to apply for a residence order or a contact order in respect of any 'child of the family'. Many step-parents, therefore, will be able to seek such orders without leave.
- Any person with whom the child has lived for at least three years has the right to apply for a residence order or a contact order (the three year period need not be continuous, but it must not have begun more than five years before the application and must not have ended more than three months before). This, like the exceptions which follow, is drawn from the existing law of custodianship, which allows 'three year carers' to apply for custody. It will be recalled that those who have cared for the child for less than three years will need the consent of the local authority, as well as the leave of the court, if they are local authority foster parents.
- Any person who has the consent of those holding an existing residence order in respect of the child is entitled to apply for a residence order or a contact order.
- Any person who has the consent of the local authority, in a case where a care order has been made, is entitled to apply for a residence order.
- Any person who has the consent of each of those who have parental responsibility for the child (on which see Chapter 2) is entitled to apply for a residence order or a contact order.

In each of the above cases, there are thought to be good reasons why the procedural barrier of having to obtain leave should be lifted.

Further exceptions may emerge, however, in relation to non-parental applications, for the Government has taken powers under the Act to make regulations specifying categories of case and categories of applicant where leave will not be needed. It is possible, for example, that at some stage in the future the Government will, in the light of experience, make regulations enabling grandparents and other types of relative to apply, without leave, for contact orders and residence orders, even if they do not fall within any of the excepted situations set out in the Act.

It goes without saying, of course, that merely because a person is exempt from the requirement of leave does not mean that they are certain to obtain the order they want. The merits of their claim will remain to be tested in accordance with the welfare principle contained in section 1 of the Act.

The effect of a section 8 order

Let us assume that a section 8 order has been made in favour of a non-parent. What are the consequences? The answer to this question will obviously depend on a number of factors. These include the type of order made, the conditions, if any, which were built into the order by the court, the type of applicant involved (step-parent, relative, foster parent, etc.) and, of course, the general circumstances of the case (e.g. whether the child was already the subject of a court order of some sort).

Contact orders will require the child's carer to permit visits to be made to the person(s) named in the order. Prohibited steps orders and specific issue orders will be directed to particular areas of contention and to that extent will be one-off measures. Residence orders are more drastic and call for separate and extended treatment.

A residence order is an order 'settling the arrangements to be made as to the person with whom a child is to live'. If such an order is made in favour of a non-parent, that person will clearly be entitled to care for the child: indeed, that is what will have been envisaged by the court. It is only right that people in this position are given the 'tools' to get on with the job and therefore the Act provides that they will have parental responsibility for the child as long as the order remains in force. Accordingly, they will have access to all the rights, powers, etc. which natural parents acquire automatically.

There are exceptions to this rule, however. Non-parents will not acquire rights in relation to the adoption of the child (i.e. the right to consent, or refuse to consent); nor will they be able to appoint a guardian for the child. These matters remain within the parents' domain. Nor will they be in a position to effect a change of name or remove the child from the UK for longer than one month unless they obtain either the written consent of every other person who has parental responsibility for the child or else the leave of the court. Those 'other persons' will include the natural parents (or, in the case of a child born outside marriage, the mother), because, as was mentioned in Chapter 2, the whole thrust of the Children Act is that parents remain parents in the eyes of the law, and so retain their responsibility, until such time as the child is adopted.

Whilst the natural parents will retain parental responsibility – and in fact share it with the holder of the residence order – their ability to exercise it may well be diminished by the rule that they must not do any act which would be incompatible with the court's order. So if the court grants a residence order to foster parents, or to a relative, the natural parents must take care not to interfere with this arrangement (unless there is agreement all round). They may, of course, be entitled to have the child visit or stay with them in accordance with a contact order. If a step-parent is granted a residence order following marriage to a natural parent, the position will obviously be rather different: they will be living with a natural parent and the order will presumably have been sought, not because of any dispute, but in order to cement the new relationships. Consequently, one would expect the residence order to be made by the court in favour of the step-parent and his or her spouse jointly. Following on from this, it is perhaps worth noting that the flexibility of the Act is such that it would be possible for the court to make a residence order in favour of both a natural parent and a non-parent who do not live together, i.e. an order whereby the child's home is to be divided.

Applications by children for section 8 orders

The wording of section 10 of the Children Act ('on the application of a person') permits children to apply for section 8 orders in respect of themselves. This is deliberate. The Gillick case in 1985 gave a much-needed boost to the law's recognition of the older child's right to self-determination and the Children Act contains a number of provisions which reflect this movement. We have already seen how the welfare checklist in section 1 refers to the ascertainable wishes and feelings of the child. Section 10 maintains this theme.

Children do not fall within the categories of persons who are entitled as of right to apply for a section 8 order. They will accordingly need to obtain leave to apply from the court and the Act provides that the court may only grant leave to a child if it is satisfied that he or she has sufficient understanding to make the proposed application. There is no fixed age laid down by the Act on this point.

Will children use the Act in this way? In so far as they have been known to intervene in legal proceedings before (e.g. by making themselves wards of court), the answer must be yes, but only on very rare occasions. No matter how much they may be supported by others, children initiating legal action in relation to their own upbringing will need immense reserves of courage, confidence and resilience to see the thing through. It would be rash to predict the sort of cases which are most likely to occur; but an example was given during the Parliamentary debates on the Act of a situation in which an application might be made. It was suggested that a child who objects to being known by a new surname or being taken abroad could apply to the court for a prohibited steps or specific issue order to prevent it.

One obvious question that will be asked is: how will the child know of his position under the Act? The answer is that where legal proceedings are already in train, his views should automatically be sought and at that stage information can be imparted. This is a function which the social worker assigned to the case (assuming there is one) may well feel is an appropriate one to discharge, but of course so much depends on the precise circumstances. In other cases, the answer to the question is that it is probably a matter of chance whether the child will come to appreciate what the courts can offer by way of help. This problem of lack of knowledge is, of course, not confined to applications made by children.

Applications by local authorities and voluntary organisations

The wording of section 10 enables applications to be made by these bodies, except that it is made clear that local authorities cannot obtain residence or contact orders. Leave should not be a problem in these cases.

Other aspects of non-parental applications

Many of the supplementary provisions mentioned in the last chapter apply equally to non—parental cases. Those worth noting are as follows:

- Section 8 orders can only be made in respect of a child over sixteen where the circumstances are exceptional.
- Section 8 orders will cease to have effect when the child reaches the age of sixteen, unless the court orders otherwise.

- All section 8 orders may be varied or discharged by the court.
- Section 8 orders are automatically discharged if a care order is later made.
- The special provisions aimed at curbing delays in legal proceedings are fully applicable.
- Family assistance orders may be made by the court, whether or not it makes a section 8 order. The person to be assisted may be a parent or guardian, anyone who is caring for the child or who holds a contact order, or the child himself.
- The court has the power to order that no further application is to be made in respect of the child without its consent. Many non-parental applicants need leave anyway, of course, but as we have seen, some do not. This provision can be used by the court to stop repeated applications by members of this group.
- No application can be made for a section 8 order, other than a residence order, in respect of a care order child. If a residence order is made, it has the effect of discharging the care order (see Chapter 10).

Financial provision for the child's carer

The existing provisions of the Children Act 1975 enable a custodian to apply for a maintenance order against the child's parents. They also enable local authorities to make payments to custodians. The 1989 Act continues these arrangements although some adjustments have been made necessary by the abolition of custodianship as a distinct legal concept. What the Act does (in Schedule 1) is enable an application for financial provision to be made against the parents (and this includes a step-parent who has treated the child as a child of the family) by the holder of a residence order. In addition, local authorities are authorised to 'make contributions towards the cost of the accommodation and maintenance of the child' to any person with whom a child lives, or is to live, as the result of a residence order. Step-parents, however, are excluded from this facility (as they are under the custodianship law).

Both the power of the court to make a financial provision order and the power of the local authority to make contributions are clearly discretionary. Their exercise in any particular case will be dependent upon the precise facts.

5 Local authority support for children and families

The scope of the present chapter

The title of this chapter is rather vague. What is 'support'? Local authorities could be said to 'support' children and their families in dozens of different ways, ranging from the provision of libraries to the inspection of shops. The title is in fact taken from Part III of the Children Act, which contains an assortment of provisions – some general, some specific – whose unifying theme is the involvement of social services departments in child welfare work. Some of these provisions are drawn from existing legislation, others are new. Some of them impose obligations on local authorities, others merely give them powers exercisable at their discretion.

It might be thought that with a title such as this, Part III of the Act would contain virtually everything in the measure concerning local authorities and children. This is not the case, however: later parts of the Act deal, inter alia, with care orders, supervision orders, emergency protection orders, community homes and the regulation of private fostering, all of them areas with a high degree of local authority involvement. To that extent, therefore, the title is misleading.

The diversity of the contents of Part III would make a single chapter devoted to all of it a rather unwieldy affair. Its coverage in this book has therefore been split. Those sections which deal with the provision of accommodation for children – what is at present commonly referred to as 'voluntary care' – are described in Chapter 6, while those sections which deal with the treatment of children who are the subject of a care order (for they also appear in Part III) are described in the care order chapter (Chapter 10). The present chapter is concerned with the remaining provisions. Hiving off segments of this part of the Act for separate treatment is probably inconsistent with the intentions of both the draftsman and the Department of Health. This is, perhaps, particularly so as far as the provision of accommodation is concerned, because the whole thrust of the Government's approach to 'voluntary care' arrangements has been that they are merely one of a number of support services which are available from local authorities to families living in their area. Nevertheless, it is hoped that through this division, the reader will be in a better position to acquire a command of what the Act has to say.

Children in need

A notable feature of Part III of the Children Act is its recurring reference to 'children in need'. Great care must be taken with this new statutory expression. It is couched in ordinary language and the general idea conveyed by it is fairly clear; but it is not what it seems, because it comes along with a definition. In other words, it is not to be taken literally; it is a legal term of art which bears a restricted meaning whenever it appears in the Act. It is extremely important to remember this. A failure to read Part III with the definition firmly in mind will probably take the reader along the wrong track.

It is easy to miss the definition, because it only appears once in the Act, in section 17(10). The definition is as follows:

a child shall be taken to be in need if –
(a) he is unlikely to achieve or maintain, or to have the opportunity of achieving or maintaining, a reasonable standard of health or development without the provision for him of services by a local authority under this Part;
(b) his health or development is likely to be significantly impaired, or further impaired, without the provision for him of such services; or
(c) he is disabled

Three of the words used in section 17(10) are themselves defined. A child is 'disabled' if he is blind, deaf or dumb or suffers from mental disorder of any kind or is substantially and permanently handicapped by illness, injury or congenital deformity or such other disability as may be prescribed by regulations. 'Development' means physical, intellectual, emotional, social or behavioural development. 'Health' means physical or mental health.

One of the first things which many will notice about this definition of children in need is its inclusion of the handicapped. This is a manifestation of the policy, originally proposed in the Child Care Law Review and subsequently adopted by the Department of Health, of unifying the two existing main streams of public child law; these have been described as child care law on the one hand and health and welfare law on the other. The first is to be found largely in the Child Care Act 1980, many of whose provisions date back to the Children Act 1948. The second is scattered throughout various pieces of legislation covering not just children but people of all age groups, e.g. the National Assistance Act 1948 and the Chronically Sick and Disabled Persons Act 1970. Child care law, understood in the above sense, embraces the voluntary reception of children ('orphans and deserted children, etc.', in the words of the Child Care Act) into local authority care, but it also contains a strong preventive element whereby children living at home with their families are supported by the local authority. Health and welfare law opens up similar possibilities – support at home and care away from home – but the rules which apply are completely separate from, and arguably inferior to, the rules relating to child care. The DoH view is that this dichotomy cannot be justified and that a merger of the two streams of law will have positive advantages. This view is reflected in Part III of the Children Act and particularly in the definition of 'children in need'.

It is worth noting that the Government's policy has not gone unchallenged. In its 1987 White Paper, the DoH referred to:

> the reservations expressed by some that this would cause concern to those parents of handicapped and disabled children who provide expert and devoted care but from time to time need respite care provided by the local authority. This concern it was said flowed from the perception that reception into care by local authorities under the present legislation was frequently associated with parental shortcomings.

However, the Government held to its view, no doubt fortified by the support it got from organisations representing the handicapped. 'The intention', it said, 'is to ensure that in all cases the children concerned receive the standard of care and protection and professional review appropriate to their needs and that those ends are achieved where possible in a partnership with parents.'

A further, important, feature of the definition which should be noted is its inclusion of children who are likely to encounter difficulties, as well as those who already have them. The wording of paragraphs (a) and (b) of the definition makes this clear. As was said in Parliament, 'one has to see the child in his or her particular situation and ask: "Well, if nothing is done for that child by the local authority, is that child likely to attain a reasonable standard of development?" ' This is a very good example of the need to have the definition in mind when operating the Act, because without it, it would be a matter of doubt as to whether the words 'child in need' were sufficient to cover such children. Through its reference to likelihood, however, the definition puts the matter beyond doubt and paves the way for important preventive functions to be given to local authorities.

It should also be noted that the definition is sufficiently broad to encompass children who are already in local authority care, as well as children living outside. This, another example of the extended meaning of 'child in need', paves the way for rehabilitative work to be done.

The creation of this statutory group of 'children in need' has provoked mixed reactions. Some have sought to argue that, while it is undoubtedly well—intentioned, it will produce problems of interpretation (consider the precision, or lack of precision, in the definition) and, equally importantly, will produce an unfortunate labelling effect. It has been suggested that identifying a child as one 'in need' will reinforce negative feelings and lock the family into a 'stigmatised framework'. No doubt there is some force in this line of argument. The Government's response, however, is that the definition will set a target for local authorities to aim for. As there will not be limitless resources available, services under Part III of the Act must be targeted on those in greatest need. This is, of course, a familiar argument these days.

The provision of services for children and families

The Children Act aims to set out the functions of local authority social services departments in relation to children in need. Given this aim, and given the special meaning which the term 'child in need' bears in the Act, it is not surprising to find a fairly long list of functions. What *is* perhaps surprising is the fact that these functions are not all laid out in the same corner of the statute. In order to make his work more intelligible, the draftsman has decided to place at the forefront of Part III a section (section 17) which contains the *general duty* of local authorities. This is then supplemented, or filled out, by a number of *specific duties and powers* which have been consigned to Schedule 2, at the back of the Act.

Not everyone will agree with this sort of arrangement – there was certainly opposition to it in Parliament – but that is the way the Act has turned out. It is important to remember that the provisions in a schedule of a statute are just as much law as the provisions in the sections. It is understandable how a schedule can come to be regarded as something akin to a second-tier form of law, but such an approach is misconceived. Certainly it would be a great mistake to look upon the contents of Schedule 2 of the Children Act as something peripheral; many would regard them as being among the most important provisions in the Act.

The general duty of the local authority

> It shall be the general duty of every local authority (a) to safeguard and promote the welfare of children within their area who are in need, and (b) so far as is consistent with that duty, to promote the upbringing of such children by their families, by providing a range and level of services appropriate to those children's needs.

This is how section 17(1) of the Act reads. Inspired by the existing section 1 of the Child Care Act 1980, it is a provision of the very highest significance, opening up as it does a vast array of child-oriented social services work. The prime duty is that contained in paragraph (a). Paragraph (b) is a reflection of the view that, generally speaking, the interests of children are best served by their remaining with their families, but this is only generally speaking and so the Act does not require the local authority to promote this where it would be inconsistent with the child's welfare.

The section envisages that the duty will be discharged by the provision of an 'appropriate' range of services. At first sight, it seems as though the provision must come from the local authority, but section 17 goes on to state that the authority may make arrangements for others to act on its behalf. Furthermore, it is required to 'facilitate' the provision by others, including in particular voluntary organisations, of relevant services. This is a statutory acknowledgement of the very great part that voluntary bodies play in family support work. The extent of joint action by the local authority and the voluntary sector is left to be arranged locally, so variations will occur.

The problem with a statutory provision like section 17(1) is that its language is so open. What *are* the services which are to be provided? What exactly does 'appropriate' mean? What will promote the welfare of children in need (as defined)? The short answer to such questions is that there is no single right answer. The reality is that section 17(1), though couched in the language of duty, gives local authorities a very considerable degree of discretion in deciding what, if anything, to do. The duty is, in a sense, more political than legal. This is not to say that it has no place in a Children Act. Clearly, the point it is making is fundamental. It is just that, as a vehicle for ensuring that things get done (and get done consistently throughout the country), its value is limited. It leaves a great deal – and some might say too much – to the will and determination of those in charge of the local authority. But this may be an unfair argument. After all, section 17(1) is only a lead-in to the specific duties and powers set out in Schedule 2. What of them?

The specific duties and powers in Schedule 2

Schedule 2 contains ten sets of provisions, each of which is seen as furthering in its own way the overall objective established by section 17(1). There is provision in the Act for the Government, with Parliament's approval, to amend these provisions, so that the legislation can reflect any new social services practices which may develop in the future in relation to children in need. The ten matters dealt with are as follows:

Identification of children in need and the provision of information

Every local authority is required to take reasonable steps to identify the extent to which there are children in need (remember the special definition) within its area. It must also publish information about the services relevant to such children which it provides and, where appropriate, which others – including in particular voluntary organisations – provide. It must take such steps as are reasonably practicable to ensure that those who might benefit from the services receive the information relevant to them.

Maintenance of a register of disabled children

Every local authority is required to keep a register of disabled children within its area. We have seen that section 17 of the Act contains a definition of 'disabled'.

Assessment of children's needs

The local authority may assess the needs of any child who appears to be 'in need' within the meaning of section 17 at the same time as any assessment is carried out under other legislation (e.g. the Education Act 1981).

Prevention of neglect and abuse

Every local authority is required to take reasonable steps, through the provision of services, to prevent children within its area suffering ill-treatment or neglect. 'Ill-treatment' is defined elsewhere in the Act so as to include sexual abuse and forms of ill-treatment which are not physical (e.g. emotional abuse). If a local authority believes that a child within its area is likely to suffer harm but lives or proposes to live in another local authority's area, it must inform the other authority.

Provision of accommodation to protect children

Where it appears to a local authority that a child is suffering, or is likely to suffer, ill-treatment at the hands of another person who is living with him, and that other person proposes to move from the premises, the authority is empowered to assist with the obtaining of alternative accommodation. This was a late addition to the Act which arose out of the debates on emergency protection orders. It is discussed in Chapter 8 (see page 89).

Provision for disabled children

Every local authority is required to provide services designed to minimise the effect on disabled children within its area of their disabilities and to give such children the opportunity to lead lives which are as normal as possible.

Provisions to reduce the need for legal proceedings

Every local authority is required to take reasonable steps designed to reduce the need to bring proceedings for care or supervision orders with respect to children within its area, or criminal proceedings against them, or wardship proceedings, or any family proceedings which might lead to them being placed in the authority's care. It is also required to take steps designed to encourage children within its area not to commit criminal offences and steps designed to avoid the need for children to be placed in secure accommodation.

Provision for children living with their families

Every local authority is required to make such provision as it considers appropriate for the following services to be available with respect to children in need within its area while they are living with their families: (a) advice, guidance and counselling; (b) occupational, social, cultural or recreational activities; (c) home help; (d) facilities for, or assistance with, travelling to and from home for the purpose of taking advantage of any other service provided under the Act or of any similar service; (e) assistance to enable the child concerned and his family to have a holiday.

Family centres

Every local authority is required to provide such family centres as it considers appropriate in relation to children within its area. A 'family centre' for these purposes is a centre at which the child, his parents and any other person who has parental responsibility for him (e.g. the holder of a residence order) or who is looking after him, may (a) attend for occupational, social, cultural or recreational activities; (b) attend for advice, guidance or counselling; or (c) be provided with accommodation while he is receiving advice, guidance or counselling.

Maintenance of the family home

Every local authority is required to take reasonable steps, where any child in need within its area is living apart from his family, to enable him to live with his family or to promote contact between him and his family, if, in its opinion, it is necessary to do so in order to safeguard or promote his welfare. This duty does not extend to children in local authority accommodation (other provisions cover them).

These are wide-ranging and ambitious provisions and will enable a great deal of supportive, preventive and rehabilitative work to be continued by local authorities, in conjunction with voluntary organisations and others. Some of the provisions will strike a familiar chord – the seventh, for example, which is partly based on section 1 of the Child Care Act 1980 (itself a repetition of section 1 of the Children and Young Persons Act 1963). As with section 17(1), however, although the language of duty is employed extensively, the qualifications inserted – 'as they consider appropriate' – and the bland nature of many of the duties – 'shall take reasonable steps' – will ensure that local authorities retain a large measure of freedom to decide how exactly the functions in question will be discharged. The range, and level, of services will consequently vary from area to area, with different matters being given different priorities. Nor does the Act regulate in any way the manner in which social work support is to be delivered. Different practices will therefore continue to flourish.

The question is sometimes asked about public duties of this sort, what can be done if the local authority fails to discharge them? In recent years, much has been accomplished by the High Court by way of improving and extending its special jurisdiction of 'judicial review' over public agencies. In principle, this jurisdiction is available for the enforcement of public duties. Cases have shown, however, that the judges are reluctant to intervene in situations which involve duties framed in less than very specific language. Such cases often contain controversial political elements, such as the allocation of scarce resources, which the courts are understandably wary of. In an extreme set of circumstances, where say a local authority has done nothing at all to implement a duty, a judge might be prepared to act. Otherwise, the tendency, so far as broad duties are concerned, is to leave the matter to the authority's discretion. As a result, 'enforcement' can only be pursued through whatever non-legal channels might be available.

It was suggested during the Parliamentary debates on the Act that the Government should be given power to establish minimum standards for local authorities in relation to their work under Schedule 2. This was resisted. Local authorities, it was said, are accountable to their local electorate and are responsible for making their own decisions according to their priorities and the particular needs and circumstances of their area. This is one matter, then, on which central government is prepared to adopt a hands-off approach. Such support for local government autonomy may be warmly welcomed, but the fear in some quarters is that it will only serve to perpetuate perceived inadequacies in some of the country's social services departments.

What the Government did agree to, however, was the inclusion in the Act of a provision giving the DoH a 'default power'. This is contained in section 84 of the Act. It enables the Secretary of State to declare a local authority to be in default with respect to any duty imposed by the Act, and to give directions (enforceable in the High Court) for the purpose of ensuring that the duty is complied with. The power can only be exercised where the Department is satisfied that the local authority has failed, without reasonable excuse, to comply with the duty in question. Experience of default powers in other fields (e.g. education) shows that government departments use them very infrequently. They are rather heavy-handed instruments, with a considerable potential for exacerbating delicate central-local relationships. Those thinking of utilising this particular complaints machinery should bear this in mind.

A more fruitful option, perhaps, will be the internal complaints procedure which each local authority will have to establish under section 26 of the Act. This procedure, discussed in Chapter 6, will be available to all children in need and their families, whether or not the children are being looked after by the authority, and as we have just seen, several of the functions specified in Schedule 2 are aimed directly at them.

Assistance in kind and assistance in cash

Section 17(6) states that the services provided by a local authority in the exercise of its functions in relation to children in need 'may include giving assistance in kind or, in exceptional circumstances, in cash'. This power is not new, as it already exists under the Child Care Act 1980, and existed before that under the Children and Young Persons Act 1963. There are, however, some new supplementary provisions: first, assistance may be unconditional or subject to conditions as to the repayment of the assistance or of its value (in whole or in part); second, the means of the child and his parents must be taken into account before assistance is given or conditions imposed; and third, no repayment will be due from a person at a time when he is in receipt of income support or family credit.

The power of a local authority to provide this sort of assistance has unquestionable value. But the high discretionary element means that problems over its implementation are inevitable. Three matters in particular were highlighted in the debate on the Children Act, each of them concerned with cash payments: the enormous variations which exist between local authorities, the low amount of the average payment, and the misunderstandings – in essence, unwarranted rigidity – of social workers caused by the use of the expression 'exceptional circumstances'. These points were all accepted by the Government but, basing its case on the recommendations of the Child Care Law Review, it argued that the existing statutory wording was the best formula available. It was especially reluctant to see the 'exceptional circumstances' criterion disappear, on the grounds that relaxation could push local authorities into an income maintenance role which is more properly assigned to the social security system.

Day care for the under fives and supervision of school children

Section 18 of the Children Act deals with the important question of day care. Opinions obviously vary as to the extent to which public authorities should have obligations in this area and so the terms of the section were always going to be contentious. In the result, the Act draws a distinction between children in need (as defined) and other children.

As regards children in need, the section imposes a duty on the local authority to provide (and this can be done through other organisations) such day care for those aged five or under who are not yet attending school as is appropriate. 'Day care' for these purposes is defined as 'any form of care or supervised activity provided for children during the day (whether or not it is provided on a regular basis)'. Under Schedule 2 of the Act, a local authority, in making these arrangements, must have regard to the different racial groups to which children who are in need within its area belong. This interesting provision is clearly designed to ensure that all sections of the community are properly catered for (see also Chapter 19).

A similar duty extends to those children attending school: every local authority is required to provide for children in need within its area who are attending any school 'such care or supervised activities as is appropriate' outside school hours or during school holidays. 'Supervised activity' means an activity supervised by a responsible person.

As regards children other than those 'in need', section 18 refers to a *discretion* to provide day care or supervised activities. Whether or not any initiative is launched is accordingly a matter for each individual authority.

The provisions of section 18 give a higher statutory profile to day care and will enable many imaginative schemes to be devised and supported. In this sense, they represent a step forward. An important question remains, however: will the necessary political will, together with the release of adequate resources, be forthcoming? It is true that in relation to children in need, the Act imposes obligations on authorities, not simply discretions. These obligations, moreover, are framed in objective terms ('as is appropriate' and not, as in the initial version of the Children Bill, 'as they consider appropriate'). As with section 17 and Schedule 2, though, it is difficult to see coercive measures being taken against an individual authority. The Government seemed to accept this during the Parliamentary debates.

In an attempt to keep local authorities on their toes, however, the Government put into the Act a section (section 19) which requires each authority to review the provision which it makes under section 18. These reviews are to be conducted with the education department and are to take place at fixed intervals (or more frequently if desired). The first review is to take place within a year of the implementation of the Act; further reviews are to occur every three years. The form a review takes is a matter for the authorities concerned, but they are bound to 'have regard to' (this does not mean accept) any representations made by a health authority and any other relevant representations. And once the review is concluded, the results, together with any proposals, must be published as soon as is reasonably practicable.

It should be noted that sections 18 and 19 do not deal simply with local authority provision. They also contain rules concerning the provision of day care by the private sector. These rules are described in Chapter 16.

Charges for local authority services

Section 29 of the Act enables a local authority to charge for any service it provides under section 17 or section 18, other than advice, guidance and counselling. Those who can be charged are the child's parents, the child himself (if 16 or over) and any member of the child's family if the service is in fact provided to that person with a view to promoting the child's welfare. There is power to waive part or all of the charge where the means of the payer are deemed insufficient and in any event no-one is liable to pay at a time when he is receiving income support or family credit.

Co-operation between authorities

In an attempt to ensure a properly co-ordinated approach by public agencies, section 27 of the Act expressly authorises local authorities to request help from other councils and from health authorities in the discharge of their functions under Part III. The agency whose help is sought is under an obligation to comply with a request 'if it is compatible with their own statutory or other duties and does not unduly prejudice the discharge of any of their functions'. Inter-agency co-operation, like co-operation between individuals, is difficult to achieve by legal methods alone (a matter discussed in Chapter 7). To an extent, therefore, and bearing in mind the rather loose language which it employs, section 27 is another of the Children Act's more symbolic provisions.

What the Act does not do

In his important recent book *Putting Families First* (1988), Mac-millan, Bob Holman makes the point that an effective preventative strategy does not simply entail the imposition of duties on social services departments. It involves much wider issues, such as the redistribution of wealth, income support and housing, and it involves institutions other than social services departments: central government, other departments within social services authorities, local authorities other than social services authorities (e.g. district councils), voluntary organisations and social work training establishments all have a part to play. The Children Act does not purport to tackle all of these matters. The Government emphasised time and again during the Parliamentary debates that the Act was neither a social security Act nor a housing Act. So far as Part III of the Act is concerned, the emphasis is very firmly on the functions of social services departments. As a result, it is vulnerable to criticism from those who are keen on a preventative approach in the broadest sense of that term. They will no doubt view the Act as being only a partial corrective to urgent and deep-seated social problems.

6 Provision of accommodation for children

The new philosophy

There can be little doubt that section 20 will take its place among the better known provisions of the Children Act. It is designed to replace the existing legislation, set out mainly in section 2 of the Child Care Act 1980, governing the reception of children into so-called 'voluntary care', a process which embraces some 20,000 children each year.

Section 20 is located in Part III of the Act, which, as was seen in the last chapter, is entitled 'Local Authority Support for Children and Families'. Its appearance there, alongside sections dealing with preventive and supportive services and day care, is indicative of the approach which commended itself to the Child Care Law Review and subsequently to the Department of Health. This approach sees the provision by a local authority of accommodation for children as a valuable service which should be on offer, on a wholly voluntary basis, to families in difficulties, in exactly the same way as its other Part III services are. Using the accommodation service should, according to this view, be regarded positively, as a means of assisting the child; it should not be looked upon as evidence of parental failure but as evidence of a responsible attitude to the discharge of parental duties. The existing legislation is considered vulnerable to criticism through casting voluntary care in too negative a light: witness section 1 of the Child Care Act, which talks of promoting the welfare of children by diminishing the need to receive children into care. Wording of this sort, it is said, conveys the wrong impression, the impression that being accommodated by the local authority is something to be avoided at all costs.

This emphasis on accommodation as a service, entered into freely with the child's family, has a number of implications but the most important is the elimination of all traces of compulsion from the service – no obstacles are to be placed in the way of families wishing to use it. If compulsory intervention is deemed necessary, then a court order must be obtained on one of the grounds set out in a completely separate part of the statute (Part IV). It is interesting to note that in order to emphasise the split with the compulsory procedure, separate terminology has been introduced: when the Children Act comes into force, children 'in care' will be those who are the subject of a care order made by the court, whereas children dealt with under section 20 will simply be 'accommodated'.

The powers and duties under section 20

The principal accommodation obligation imposed by the Act is contained in section 20(1). It reads as follows:

> Every local authority shall provide accommodation for any child in need within their area who appears to them to require accommodation as a result of – (a) there being no person who has parental responsibility for him; (b) his being lost or having been abandoned; or (c) the person who has been caring for him being prevented (whether or not permanently, and for whatever reason) from providing him with suitable accommodation or care.

This provision is very similar to section 2 of the Child Care Act 1980. One difference, however, is its reference to children in need. The obligation is only owed to these children. As was seen in the last chapter, 'child in need' is a term with a special meaning and covers not simply those in what might be called social need, but also those who are disabled. This latter group of children is therefore brought into mainstream child care law instead of being dealt with alongside adults in the health legislation. 'Parental responsibility' bears the meaning given to it by Part I of the Act (discussed in Chapter 2) and so paragraph (a) would normally refer to the natural parents of the child, or the mother if the child was born outside marriage. Finally, it will be noticed that the duty extends to children in need of any age – it is not restricted to those under seventeen, as is the duty under the 1980 Act.

In addition to creating the main duty in subsection (1), section 20 contains two other measures authorising the provision of accommodation. The first (subsection (3)) covers children in need aged sixteen or over whose welfare is considered 'likely to be seriously prejudiced' if accommodation is not provided. It is in fact cast as a duty, not just a discretion, and it appears in the Act as a result of uncertainty on the Government's part as to the extent of a parent's legal duty to accommodate a child who has reached the age of sixteen. To meet this possible problem, it has been decided to provide a local authority safety net for children of this age group who are not living at home. As with section 20(1), this is a service which is to be on offer, and so the child will not be compelled to accept it.

The other accommodation provision in section 20 is subsection (4). This enables (not requires) a local authority to provide accommodation for any child – whether 'in need' or not – if it considers that to do so would safeguard or promote his welfare, even though there is a person with parental responsibility who is able to accommodate him. Runaways would be covered by this power.

The parental veto

The accommodation service under section 20 is seen as a voluntary one. Hence:

> A local authority may not provide accommodation under this section for any child if any person who (a) has parental responsibility for him; and (b) is willing and able to (i) provide accommodation for him; or (ii) arrange for accommodation to be provided for him, objects (section 20(7)).

So the parents have a veto, as they do at present. This fundamental rule, however, will not apply in two situations. The first is where the child is over sixteen and agrees to being provided with the accommodation. Here we have yet another illustration of the self-determination principle at work and the result of it is that a sixteen or seventeen year old may admit himself to care if the statutory conditions are satisfied.

The second situation in which a parent is denied a veto is where a residence order has been made under section 8 of the Act (or a care and control order has been made in wardship proceedings) and the holder of the order agrees to the provision of accommodation. The holder might be one of the parents themselves, but he might also be a relative, or a foster parent. In any event, the parent without the order will be unable to stop the holder arranging accommodation. This is a perfectly logical rule, because the central purpose of a residence order is to give the holder the exclusive power to decide where the child is to live. This can obviously include local authority accommodation.

It should also be noted that a veto is only given to a parent who is willing and able to provide or arrange for accommodation for the child. This qualification was inserted into the Act so as to prevent an estranged parent frustrating the other, caring, parent's plan to use

the section 20 service by lodging an objection even though he himself
had no intention of taking in the child. To deny the caring parent the
service in these circumstances was thought to be wrong.

As far as children born outside marriage are concerned, normally
only the mother will have a veto. This is because only she will have
parental responsibility. If the father has acquired parental responsibility in any of the ways mentioned in Chapters 2 and 3, it is a
different matter.

Can the provision of accommodation be demanded?

Suppose a parent asks the local authority to provide accommodation
under section 20(1) but the local authority refuses. Does the parent
have any redress? It is true that, as a matter of strict law, section
20(1) is framed in terms of a duty rather than a discretion. This
might suggest that legal enforcement is available. The problem is
that the duty only arises where the child 'appears to them' – i.e. the
local authority – to require accommodation. Moreover, obtaining
judicial enforcement would necessitate the parent showing that,
contrary to the opinion of the authority, all the relevant conditions,
such as the child being 'in need', were satisfied. This would be no
easy task. Probably the most that can be said is that if the local
authority refuses accommodation for a wholly extraneous and
irrelevant reason, the court might intervene on the application of an
aggrieved party (and this could include the child himself in
appropriate cases). But in any event, going to court (and in this type
of situation it would have to be by way of the special judicial review
procedure in the High Court in London) is a very cumbersome and
wearying business. It often creates more problems than it solves. It
is, perhaps, a shade unrealistic to expect dissatisfied individuals to
regard it as a viable method of achieving their objective. The
exertion of pressure on management, members of the social services
committee, Members of Parliament and the Department of Health is
likely to prove more efficacious in many cases. Nor should it be
forgotten that the local authority's complaints procedure may be
available (see below).

Does the child have a say?

We have already seen that the parental veto disappears if the child is
over sixteen and he agrees to being provided with accommodation.
This right to self-determination does not extend to the under
sixteens. If a child under sixteen expresses a wish to go into

accommodation, but the parents disagree, compulsory powers will be needed if the child is to move. This will involve the local authority going to court and proving grounds for an order.

What of the child who opposes the idea of local authority care? The Children Act does not require the child's consent to be obtained before section 20 accommodation is provided. What it does do is require the child's views to be considered:

> Before providing accommodation under this section, a local authority shall, so far as is reasonably practicable and consistent with the child's welfare – (a) ascertain the child's wishes regarding the provision of accommodation; and (b) give due consideration (having regard to his age and understanding) to such wishes of the child as they have been able to ascertain (section 20(6)).

Although the Act does not give the child a veto, in practice a veto there will certainly be – at any rate for the older child of sixteen or seventeen who can leave school and become self-supporting. The reason for this is that there is nothing to stop such a child leaving the accommodation which has been provided. To acquire the power to detain him, the local authority will need a court order granted under the compulsory provisions of the Act; if there are no grounds available for an order, and there may well not be any if the child has suitable alternative accommodation to go to, then the local authority is not really in a position to do anything. As was said by a Government minister in Parliament, the over-sixteens 'can always vote with their feet'. It was for this reason that no specific provision on the matter was included in the Act.

The position when accommodation is provided

The code of treatment

Once a child is provided with accommodation under section 20, there becomes applicable an important series of provisions in the Children Act covering all children who are, to use the words of the Act, 'looked after by a local authority'. The other major group of children caught by this expression consists of those who are subject to a care order. In so far as the Act lays down a code of treatment common to those in care under both voluntary and compulsory arrangements, it is no different from the existing law set out in the Child Care Act 1980. Indeed, there is also considerable similarity as far as the details of the code are concerned, since many of the provisions have been lifted straight out of the 1980 Act. The opportunity has been taken, however, of introducing some signifi- cant changes. The code of treatment is contained partly in sections

20–29 of the Act and partly in Schedule 2. Set out below is a commentary on the main features of this code, looked at from the particular perspective of the child in section 20 accommodation and his family.

Matters on which there is no great change

● The general duty of a local authority remains the same: to safeguard and promote the child's welfare (section 22(3)). The following observation from the Government may serve to put this laudable provision into some perspective:

> it must be recognised that local authorities have to discharge their legal responsibilities within the limits of the resources available, so that the best for any individual child or group of children may simply not be available or available only at considerable cost to other children or to other client groups whose needs may be just as great

● The local authority is to make such use of services available for children cared for by their own parents as appears reasonable (also section 22(3)).

● The duty to ascertain the wishes and feelings of the child before making any decision concerning him, and to give due consideration to them, is retained (section 22(4)).

● The local authority continues to have power to take measures to protect the public even though they may be inconsistent with its general duty (section 22(6).

● The local authority continues to have discretion in the type of accommodation it provides (section 23(2)). No preference of any sort is indicated in the Act. Two small changes are worth noting, however. Firstly, the provision relating to fostering refers, not to the child being boarded out, in the way of the existing legislation, but to the child being placed with 'a family, a relative or any other suitable person'. The significant point here is the specific reference to relatives. The Act certainly does not compel the use of relatives for foster care; but the intention is to remind social workers of the benefits (well documented in the research) which placement within the family can produce. The second change is the appearance in the statute book of the term 'local authority foster parent'. Such a person is, generally speaking, anyone with whom a child has been placed. Although Parliamentary attempts to alter the wording to 'foster carer' met with defeat (on the grounds that this would be a premature move), there is nothing to stop this other term, which has many adherents, being used in practice if that is preferred.

● Whatever type of accommodation is provided, the local authority should ensure that it is near the child's home, so far as this is reasonably practicable and consistent with his welfare (section 23(7)). The existing Child Care Act 1980 was amended in 1983 to take in this obligation.

● The secure accommodation provisions, currently contained in section 21A of the Child Care Act, are retained with no real alteration (section 25)). So that secure accommodation (defined in the section as 'accommodation provided for the purpose of restricting liberty') may be used only if it appears (a) that the child has a history of absconding and is likely to abscond from any other description of accommodation and, if he absconds, he is likely to suffer significant harm, or (b) that if he is kept in any other description of accommodation he is likely to injure himself or other persons. The Government will continue to have power to make regulations which, inter alia, govern the duration of secure placements and enable the criteria to be tested in legal proceedings.

These provisions apply to children accommodated under voluntary arrangements just as much as to those in compulsory care. According to the Child Care Law Review:

> About 10 per cent of admissions to secure accommodation are of children received into care, who form 5 per cent of those in secure accommodation at any one point. It has been questioned whether local authorities should be able to place children presently received into care in secure accommodation. However, children in the care of local authorities may be particularly needy and vulnerable whatever the route by which they entered care, and temporary containment will in a few cases be desirable without needing to take over parental powers in order to do so.

Concerted efforts were made in Parliament to bring about a general tightening of the rules under which children can be placed in secure accommodation. In particular, it was suggested that the use of such a facility to deal with the problem of absconding from accommodation was open to abuse, and that stricter criteria should be imposed. The Department of Health's response was to urge the preservation of the existing legal framework, which it felt was needed to deal with the various types of situation which can occur. It did, however, announce that further guidance on the subject is likely to be issued to local authorities. This will stress a number of points. First, that 'decisions to make secure placements should not be taken lightly'; second, that 'wherever practicable, such decisions should be taken at a senior level within the authority'; and third, that 'before such placements are made, in addition to satisfying itself that the statutory criteria apply, the local authority should be satisfied that no other form of dealing with the case is appropriate'. The guidance will also provide examples of ways in which local authorities may 'further develop their services to reduce the need to restrict children's liberty'. This last point meshes in with the provision in

Schedule 2 of the Act (mentioned in Chapter 5) under which local authorities are required, as part of their preventive functions, to take steps designed to avoid the need for children within their area to be placed in secure accommodation.

According to section 25(9), 'this section is subject to section 20(8)'. This lapse into legalistic drafting disguises the rule that persons with parental responsibility may remove the child from secure accommodation where this has been provided in pursuance of voluntary arrangements. Not every parent will agree with the local authority having recourse to a locking-up device for their child, no matter how persuasive the social workers are, and this provision makes it clear that they have the ultimate remedy of removal at their disposal, (explored in more detail later in the present chapter).

● The **review of cases** within the local authority will continue to be subject to government regulations (section 26). The legal position here is rather complicated. Regulations on this subject have never actually been made by the Department of Health, in spite of the fact that it has had the power to do so since the Children Act 1975 was passed. Instead, local authorities have simply retained the obligation, imposed by the Children and Young Persons Act 1969, to hold a review every six months but without being subject to any detailed regulation as to the way in which such review is to be conducted. The Children Act dispenses with the six-monthly review rule and leaves everything to be covered by regulations. Consequently, when the Act is brought into force, the Government will be obliged to use its power if there is to be any legal duty to review on the part of the social services department.

The new legislation differs from that currently in place (albeit unused) by expanding on the sort of matters which the regulations might cover. Seeing that these regulations, when eventually made, are likely to mirror this list, it may be worth noting its contents. According to section 26(2), the regulations may make provision:

(a)   as to the manner in which each case is to be reviewed (the Government has said: 'we would expect most reviews to include a meeting, but that may not always be so');

(b)   as to the considerations to which the local authority is to have regard in reviewing each case;

(c)   as to the time when each case is first to be reviewed and the frequency of subsequent reviews;

(d)   requiring the authority, before conducting any review, to seek the views of the child, his parents, any non-parent having parental responsibility for him and any other person whose views the authority considers to be relevant ('it is important that all those who have an important contribu-

tion to make should be given the opportunity to do so, so
that the right decision can be made. In particular, the child,
who is central to the review, should be given the opportunity to participate appropriately. That could include attendance at the meeting. It may be advantageous that others
should attend – teachers, doctors and others – according to
the circumstances of the case');

(e)   this is concerned with care order children and will be dealt
       with in Chapter 10;

(f)   requiring the authority to consider whether the accommo-
       dation provided accords with the requirements of the Act;

(g)   requiring the authority to inform the child, so far as is
       reasonably practicable, of any steps he may take under the
       Act;

(h)   requiring the authority to make arrangements to implement
       any decision which it proposes to make as a result of the
       review (the Government has indicated that this paragraph
       is likely to be used to require the designation of a named
       social worker who will be given the task of overseeing the
       implementation of decisions taken at review: 'the child's
       welfare will be protected by a detailed and professional
       assessment of his needs and the child should thereafter be
       protected from the risk of drift by the personal attention and
       constant review of the named officer');

(i)   requiring the authority to notify details of the result of the
       review and of any decision taken by it to the child, his
       parents and others concerned.

If the Government follows and builds on the pattern established by
these paragraphs, there should be less cause for concern about the
review system. The extensive research carried out during the past
few years provides overwhelming evidence not only of substantial
variations in local authority practice but also of widespread
departures from fair and effective standards. Common sense alone
dictates that a review is a critical event for a child in care and yet we
have DoH reports concluding that in some areas reviews are either
not carried out at all or else are only carried out in a perfunctory
manner. One of the reasons for this state of affairs is the absence of
comprehensive legal regulation of the subject. The sooner the
regulations are made, therefore, the better.

● Section 29 and Schedule 2 of the Act continue the arrangements
under which parents are liable to contribute towards the maintenance of the child while he is being accommodated by the local
authority. The provisions are more or less the same as those
currently in force, and so deal with matters such as contribution
notices and court orders, but there is an addition: the Government

has taken powers to make regulations setting out the factors which local authorities are to take into account in deciding whether it is reasonable to insist on contributions and, if so, what the arrangements for payment should be. Regulations may also contain an outline of the procedures to be followed in reaching contribution agreements with parents.

The collection of contributions is not an uncontroversial matter, of course, and the case for its abolition was strongly pressed in Parliament. Perhaps not surprisingly, the Government resisted the proposal.

● Under section 23 and Schedule 2, the DoH will retain the power to make regulations concerning placements with foster parents. While the Children Act was being debated in Parliament, the Government produced a completely new set of regulations on fostering, to come into force on 1 June 1989. These regulations, made after lengthy consultations, obviously represent much of the current thinking within the DoH and one may expect them to be largely reflected in the rules made under the Children Act. Changes are possible though; for example, it may be that the new provisions will deal in a conclusive way with the controversial matter of corporal punishment. Much time was spent on this question in Parliament and in the words of the Government, 'there is everything to play for in the regulations that are to be drafted'.

● Local authorities will continue to have the power to make payments to parents and others to facilitate visits to, or by, their children (Schedule 2).

● The power of the local authority to guarantee apprenticeship deeds is retained (Schedule 2).

● The power to arrange for the child's emigration is retained by Schedule 2 of the Act. The procedure has been changed, however. The existing legislation (section 24 of the Child Care Act) requires the consent of the DoH to be obtained in each case before emigration takes place. The Children Act imposes two separate procedures, one for care order children (on which see Chapter 10) and one for those provided with accommodation. As far as the latter group are concerned, the local authority is now authorised to arrange for emigration provided it has the approval of every person who has parental responsibility for the child.

Innovatory aspects of the code of treatment

● We have seen how the Act requires the child to be consulted wherever possible with regard to decisions affecting him. It goes further than this, however, by also requiring the local authority to ascertain, where reasonably practicable, the wishes and feelings of the child's parents and any non-parent with parental responsibility, as well as others whose views the authority considers relevant. Having ascertained their wishes and feelings, the authority is obliged to give 'due consideration' to them.

Should those consulted feel that proper consideration has not been given to their views, whether they relate to a decision about the type of placement, the frequency of visits or anything else to do with the child, they are not without remedies. They can utilise the statutory complaints procedure or, if they have parental responsibility, they can simply remove the child from the accommodation. Both of these matters are considered below.

● Another new provision is section 22(5)(c). This requires the local authority to give due consideration to the child's religious persuasion, racial origin and cultural and linguistic background. The introduction of these delicate matters into the statute law is clearly welcome, serving as it does as a reminder to social workers and councillors to consider all the relevant factors in each case. As a legal instrument for forcing changes in practice, however, its potential is limited, as giving 'due consideration' is not a particularly restricting exercise. The result is that different agencies will be able to maintain very different policies on the treatment of children from minority groups while at the same time proclaiming an adherence to the terms of the legislation. For example, section 22(5)(c) certainly does not require children in care to be placed with families of the same racial group; but there is nothing to stop local authorities adopting policies along these lines if that is considered beneficial. Feelings run high on this issue, but the approach of the Children Act to it is essentially non-committal.

● Section 23(7) states that where the local authority is providing accommodation for a sibling of the child, they are to be accommodated together, so far as this is reasonably practicable and consistent with the child's welfare. The proviso at the end is important and obviously has the effect of avoiding the creation of an absolute duty to be followed in every case.

● Section 23(8) is devoted to accommodated children who are disabled – and it should be remembered that 'disabled' has a special meaning in the Act (see Chapter 5). The local authority is under an obligation to secure that the accommodation which it provides for such a child 'is not unsuitable to his particular needs', but again this is subject to the 'so far as is reasonably practicable' proviso.

● Schedule 2 of the Children Act contains provisions (in paragraph 15) which may be thought to be of considerable importance concerning the subject of access, or, to use the new terminology employed in the Act, '**contact**' between the child and his family. These provisions create a number of obligations, one general, the others specific.

The general duty is imposed on the local authority and requires it to endeavour to promote contact between the child and his parents, any non-parent having parental responsibility for him, any relative and any friend or other person connected with him, unless such contact is not reasonably practicable or consistent with his welfare. The wording of this duty is designed to serve a number of purposes. First, and most obviously, it aims to encourage in a positive fashion the promotion of links between the child and his family on the grounds that this is, in most cases, the best way of furthering the interests and welfare of the child. From this point of view, it is at one with section 23(6) of the Act, which requires the local authority to make arrangements, subject to considerations of practicability and welfare, to enable a child being looked after to live with his family or a friend.

A second purpose is to acknowledge that in some cases, contact is either not a viable proposition (because, for example, the parents have disappeared or have refused to co-operate) or not a desirable one. Hence we have the familiar words 'reasonably practicable' and 'consistent with his welfare'. The use of the word 'endeavour' is also designed for this purpose: according to the Government, it 'implies the idea of continuing to work at it in the hope that ultimately it will prevail'. This general duty will supersede those provisions contained in the 1983 Code of Practice on Access to Children in Care which relate to children in voluntary care (there are special contact rules concerning care order children and these are dealt with in Chapter 10).

The specific duties are concerned with the notification of addresses and they work in both directions. Each of the parents of the child has an obligation (underpinned by criminal penalties) to keep the authority informed of his or her address. A non-parent with parental responsibility for the child is under the same obligation. The other side of the coin is that the authority must take 'such steps as are reasonably practicable' to secure that these parties are kept informed of where the child is being accommodated (which, it will be recalled, must normally be a place near the child's home).

Access disputes concerning children in voluntary care can easily arise. As previously indicated, a dissatisfied parent will be able to use the complaints procedure which the Act requires to be set up; he will also be able to remove the child from the accommodation. A further manoeuvre which will be available (and this will apply to non-parents too) is to seek a contact order from the court under section 8 of the Act (see Chapters 3 and 4). Such proceedings, though, would do little to promote the partnership philosophy which supposedly permeates section 20 arrangements. Consequently, they should be viewed with caution.

● If communication between the child and his parents (or a non-parent with parental responsibility) is infrequent or non-existent, or if there have been no visits to them or by them for a year, the local authority must appoint an independent visitor for the child, whose function is to visit, advise and befriend the child (Schedule 2). This provision is based very largely on the existing section 11 of the Child Care Act, but whereas section 11 is only concerned with care order children, the new obligation extends to all children who are being 'looked after' by a local authority. An appointment does not have to be made, however, if it would not be in the child's best interests. Furthermore, a child with sufficient understanding is given a veto.

● One feature of the Children Act which received a particularly detailed examination in Parliament was the collection of provisions in section 26 concerning local authority **complaints procedures**. The position at present is that there is no legal requirement for a social services department to establish a formal procedure for handling complaints about child care decisions. The nearest we have come to it is the Code of Practice on Access issued by the DHSS in 1983. This encourages local authorities to develop 'clear procedures which will enable parents to pursue complaints about access and ask for decisions to be reviewed' and urges them to inform parents of the existence of such procedures. Progress has in fact been slow. Indeed, the view was expressed in Parliament that 'there is a tremendous reluctance to set up a complaints procedure in most social services departments, and even when complaints procedures exist they are rarely publicised'.

In the absence of any systematic internal machinery, parents and their children, relatives, foster parents and others with a grievance are faced with the prospect of badgering whoever they can manage to get hold of, whether it be a social worker, manager or councillor. This is clearly unsatisfactory. There are always external mechanisms, of course (e.g. the media, MPs, the courts and even the local ombudsman) but knowledge of them and of how to use them is scanty, to say the least, and their efficacy cannot always be guaranteed.

The question of complaints was considered by the House of Commons Social Services Committee and subsequently as part of the Child Care Law Review. The end product of these developments is section 26 of the Children Act. The first part of the section deals with reviews and this has already been described. Subsections (3) to (8) deal with complaints. According to these provisions, every local authority shall (so they have no choice in the matter) establish a procedure for considering any representations – this rather legalistic expression specifically includes complaints – made to it by any child it is looking after, his parent(s), any non-parent having parental responsibility, any local authority foster parent or 'such other person as the authority consider has a sufficient interest in the child's welfare to warrant his representations being considered'. This last term was put into the section in order to cover complaints from people such as relatives, doctors and teachers; it will also cover social services staff who wish to raise matters on the child's behalf.

Under the procedure, complaints and other comments may be made about 'the discharge by the authority of any of their functions under this Part in relation to the child'. 'This Part' means Part III of the Act, taken with the accompanying Schedule 2 set out at the back of the Act, so any matter mentioned in Part III or Schedule 2 can be made the subject of a complaint. Such a complaint could therefore concern the placement of the child, the treatment he is getting there, the contact arrangements which have been made, the charges which have been imposed on the parents, the depth of social work support being given, the breaking of any agreement made with the department, and so on.

Complaints under the statutory procedure can be made by a variety of adults, including foster parents. They can also be made by the child himself. Children's complaints will obviously have to be handled in an especially sensitive manner.

The need for an independent element in the complaints procedure which was advocated by the Child Care Law Review is reflected in section 26(4), which requires the local authority's procedure to provide for the participation of at least one person who is neither a member (i.e. a councillor) nor an officer of the authority. This is, in fact, all that the Children Act says about the precise mechanics of the complaints procedure. Subject to the independent person requirement, it looks as though the authority is completely free to decide who shall hear the complaint and in what manner. However, in common with so many areas covered by the Act, complaints procedures are to be regulated by government rules (to put it more accurately, section 26 authorises the Government to make rules, but there is little doubt that the power will be used) and these rules will inevitably have the effect of reducing the options open to local authorities. The content of the rules, whose aim will be to set out minimum standards, will no doubt be keenly negotiated between the Department of Health, the local authority representatives and other interested groups, but they may be expected to deal with matters such as stale or frivolous complaints and representation for the complainant and other interested parties. For good measure, the Act enables further Government regulations to be made which require local authorities to monitor the arrangements they have made. This compulsory monitoring is designed to ensure compliance with the

Government's procedural rules. Clearly, Parliament is anxious to see that there is no slippage by social services departments on this important matter.

Once a complaint has been heard, the local authority (assisted by the independent member(s)) will have to decide what to do about it. Section 26(7) imposes two obligations here. One is to have 'due regard' to the findings of those considering the complaint. This does not mean that the local authority must abide by the recommendations of the complaints panel; it simply means that the recommendations must be looked at and not ignored. The second obligation is to notify in writing, if this is practicable, the complainant, the child (if he has sufficient understanding) and such other persons as appear to be likely to be affected, of the authority's decision in the matter *and its reasons for taking that decision*, together with any action which it has taken or proposes to take. This requirement to give written reasons for a decision – albeit after a complaint has been lodged – is a great step forward in achieving procedural fairness for consumers of social services. It is a practice which has been followed for a long time by many authorities, and it is good to see it enshrined in legislation.

Another welcome feature of section 26 is subsection (8), which requires every local authority to give publicity to its complaints procedure. It will have a considerable amount of discretion here, however, since the duty is to give 'such publicity as they consider appropriate'. Much will depend on the social services department approaching the subject in the right spirit. In addition to its obligation under section 26(8) though, it is worth remembering the impact which the other aspect of section 26, concerning reviews, is likely to have here. It has already been seen that government regulations will be made regarding reviews; those regulations will, if the indicators in the Act are followed, require the authority to inform the child on review of any steps he may take under the Act. This will include the possibility of making a complaint.

Section 26 is only concerned with children who are being looked after by a local authority. The complaints procedure provisions do not therefore apply to children who are being accommodated in the private sector, unless they are being accommodated there on behalf of an authority under an agency agreement. However, the Government has given indications that the requirement to establish a complaints procedure may be incorporated in its regulations governing voluntary homes and registered children's homes. The private sector should therefore take note.

Making plans and avoiding drift

It is now accepted that the formulation of plans for children in care is vital. This applies to children being looked after under voluntary arrangements just as much as it applies to children in compulsory care under a court order. The increased emphasis on planning and permanence has been a particularly noticeable feature of social work practice in recent years and many practitioners will be expecting to see some reflection of this in the Children Act. How does the Act shape up in this respect?

One contribution the Act makes is in regard to reviews. As we have seen, section 26 enables the DoH to make regulations on this subject and the section gives some indication of the way in which the regulations will be framed. Of particular importance in the present context is the reference in section 26 to the regulations making provision as to the time when each case is first to be reviewed. For the child who is provided with section 20 accommodation, the first few weeks in care can be critical and the need for an early review is self-evident. One hopes that the review regulations, when eventually made, will deal with this need appropriately. Also of importance is the likelihood that the regulations will provide for the designation of a named social worker whose job will be to ensure the implementation of decisions. This will be an onerous task, but it is a necessary one if reviews are to achieve the central role which so many wish to see. The regulations will obviously have to deal with the situation where the designated officer moves jobs and a replacement is needed.

Another element in the planning process is the drawing up of **agreements** between the SSD and the parents. Such agreements would also serve to emphasise the partnership philosophy of section 20 arrangements, and they could clarify the respective responsibilities of the parties. Many people were expecting the Children Act to make specific provision for these. Their expectations were no doubt fired by the Government's 1987 White Paper, which said:

> Where the local authority provide for the care of a child away from home with the voluntary agreement of the parents, matters such as initial placement, schooling and access, and subsequent changes to these arrangements should be settled by mutual agreement. An arrangement under which parents will give notice that they wish to take the child back should also normally be settled by mutual agreement between the parents and the local authority in order to prepare a child for returning home. Regulations will clarify in broad terms the areas which such arrangements should cover though it is not proposed that there should be statutory child care agreements between parents and authorities

In the event, these expectations have been disappointed, in that there is no explicit reference in the Act to agreements. This is not to say, however, that the Government has abandoned the idea. The view it has taken is that provision can, and will, be made for agreements in the various sets of regulations which will be made in relation to each type of accommodation which local authorities can provide under section 20.

Accordingly, we are going to see references to agreements in the regulations governing foster care, community homes, voluntary homes, and so on. The present regulations do not contain such references – not even the new foster care regulations made in December 1988 – but they will in future.

Agreements will obviously not be possible in every case, e.g. because of incapacity on the parents' part, and the regulations will make provision for such situations. But their introduction, coupled with the strengthened review system, should serve to concentrate the minds of the parties on the future of the child. What goes into the agreement will depend on the circumstances of the case, quite apart from any compulsory features prescribed by the regulations. Flexibility will be needed to deal effectively with all the variable factors, such as the age of the child (the older he is, the greater should be his own contribution to it), the reason for accommodation being provided, the anticipated duration of care, the whereabouts and attitudes of the parents, the involvement of relatives, etc.

Needless to say, both the local authority and the parents will be expected to do their best to adhere to the terms agreed. At the end of the day, however, the agreement will not be absolutely binding. From the authority's point of view, its overriding obligation is that contained in section 22(3) of the Act – to safeguard and promote the child's welfare – and if it feels that this duty demands changes in the treatment of the child, then it should act accordingly, even if the agreement does not provide for them. From the parents' point of view, the provision of section 20 accommodation does not alter the fact that they retain parental responsibility for the child. The local authority lacks it. In the final analysis, therefore – and, as we shall see shortly, the Act expressly confirms this – the parents may bring the whole arrangement to an end simply by removing the child from the accommodation. The existence of an agreement with the social services department will not prevent this, not in law at any rate. It may be hard for social workers to swallow this, particularly in cases where the agreement has been a long time in the making, but if the essential feature of the section 20 service is its voluntariness, which it is, then there is no room for compulsion at any stage.

To summarise, then, it is through the processes of review and parent/local authority agreements that the Government sees planning taking place, both areas being covered by Department of Health regulations. How adequate a response is this? Some social workers would like to see the law going much further, by perhaps introducing specific time limits which would have the effect of forcing at some point the creation of a permanent family placement, natural or substitute. Many local authorities are following, or are proposing to follow, such a practice. Current Whitehall thinking, however, is cautious and seems to be along the lines of the comments made by the Child Care Law Review in 1985:

> We wholeheartedly support the aim of reducing drift, promoting long-term planning, and encouraging greater efforts to return children home where possible and appropriate. But we are concerned about some of the present non-statutory indicative limits adopted by local authorities when these are too rigidly used and do not allow for the many exceptions in which a return home or a permanent or long-term family placement would not be in the best interests of the individual child.

Removal from accommodation

This is one of the most problematic aspects of the Children Act. As has been pointed out, it is central to the Government's approach to section 20 accommodation that it is a support service on offer to families on a voluntary basis. This means that if those with parental responsibility for the child object, the service is not to be provided, and, as we have already seen, that is just what the Act says. The adoption of such an approach, however, must also mean that if those with parental responsibility wish to resume caring for the child, then they should be allowed to do so. And again, this is just what the Act says, in section 20(8):

> Any person who has parental responsibility for a child may at any time remove the child from accommodation provided by or on behalf of the local authority under this section.

This subsection is completely unambiguous. Putting it plainly, it means that the child's parent, or a non-parent with parental responsibility, can lawfully enter the accommodation in question at any time, seize the child and take him home. There are, however, two exceptions, which mirror those which apply to parental objections to the provision of accommodation. The first concerns children over 16, the second concerns the situation where a residence order is in force and the holder agrees to the provision of accommodation. In both sets of circumstances, section 20(8) does not apply.

The general rule contained in section 20(8) effects a substantial change in the existing law, and there lies the cause of the problem. The existing position is that where the child has been in 'voluntary care' for six months, the local authority can demand 28 days' notice of removal from a parent. This is laid down by section 13 of the Child Care Act 1980. In that 28 day period, the authority can prepare the child for a return home. It can also, though, take steps to acquire compulsory powers over the child. This 28 day rule, created amid controversy by the Children Act 1975, is being scrapped. This move was not recommended by the Review of Child Care Law, which referred to research by Olive Stevenson showing that the rule was being 'sparingly and sensibly applied'.

However, the DoH in its 1987 White Paper took the view that the 28 day rule was incompatible with the concept of voluntary partnership between local authorities and parents and should accordingly disappear. Where action to delay or prevent a return home was thought essential to protect the child from harm, it considered that the local authority's power to obtain an emergency protection order from a magistrate and the powers of the police would be a sufficient safeguard. It also envisaged that the parents and the authority would enter into an agreement at the outset about the child's upbringing and that this would deal with the question of giving notice of intended removal from accommodation. 'If the local authority cannot reach agreement on terms which they believe are in the child's best interest,' it said, 'then they can reserve the right to withdraw their services to the child and family.' Section 20(8) faithfully reflects the White Paper's approach.

Now it is true that emergency protection orders and the powers of the police will be available in cases where there is reasonable cause to believe that the child is likely to suffer significant harm. And it is also true that in many cases an agreement will have been reached with the child's parents under which they are to give so many hours' or days' notice of removal of their child. All this, however, has not satisfied a number of commentators and interested groups. What can be done if a parent, in spite of their 'agreement' with the authority, suddenly, and perhaps after a long period of care, turns up at a foster home or a children's home and demands the return of the child there and then, citing for good measure section 20(8) of the Children Act? In this sort of situation, it is not a complete answer to talk in terms of obtaining an EPO or bringing in the police: these procedures take time and statutory grounds need to be shown. Nor will it be against the law for a parent to break any agreement made with the authority: the only sanction for non-compliance will be a withdrawal of the offer of the accommodation service, hardly a satisfactory response in the situation under discussion. Some have therefore argued that a provision along the lines of the 28 day rule should be retained.

It is only fair, however, to point out the arguments in favour of the Government's approach. In the first place, the existing 28 day rule does not apply to all children in voluntary care, only to those in care for six months or more. So it is not quite correct to portray the new Act as bringing about a complete reversal of the present law. Secondly, it cannot seriously be disputed that a barrier such as the existing one is logically incompatible with the concept of a voluntary support service, no matter how much one bases the argument on the welfare of the child and the need to prepare him for a return to the family. As such, it has the capacity to discourage families from using the service. It is also worth remembering that this barrier is not encountered in private law. As was said in Parliament: 'if I leave my child with a relative and go along to pick up the child I would be surprised if I had to give 24 hours' notice. Very often I would give such notice, but there would be no requirement upon me to do so.' Why should the position be different where the child is in public accommodation?

There is no easy answer to these problems. While section 20(8) is a perfectly logical reflection of the voluntary service philosophy, difficulties are bound to arise in practice. Already, for example, it is being said that local authorities will be less inclined to offer accommodation. The prediction is that they will be even more inclined than they are now to seek compulsory powers. Furthermore, social workers and foster parents will be placed in a tricky position if a parent does turn up in inappropriate circumstances. The clear wording of the Act suggests that they must stand aside while the parent reclaims the child.

On this point, it is worth returning to consider the extreme, but by no means unknown, situation where the parent is clearly not in a fit state to care for the child, because, for example, he is heavily intoxicated. We know that an application can be made for an EPO and we know that the police can be asked to exercise their powers to prevent harm being done to the child – but can the child simply be withheld from the parent? The existing law is not at all clear, although the present writer inclines to the view that reasonable preventive measures can lawfully be taken. However, there is now a specific provision in the Children Act which may be capable of dealing with the matter. This is section 3(5). It has already been mentioned in Chapter 2 in relation to unmarried fathers but it has possibly greater relevance to the present discussion. In fact, it is likely to be a heavily debated provision, both in the courts and outside. Section 3(5) reads as follows:

> A person who does not have parental responsibility for a particular child but has care of the child may (subject to the provisions of this Act) do what is reasonable in all the circumstances of the case for the purpose of safeguarding or promoting the child's welfare.

In fielding the argument centred on the unfit but demanding parent, the Government has cited this provision to back up its claim that the social worker or foster parent, faced with an on-the-spot decision, is not powerless. Indeed, it was quite specific on the point during the Parliamentary debates:

> I consider that a foster parent would be able to prevent a parent who, by

reason of alcohol or drugs, was in no fit state to remove the child from doing so. The combination of that power [under section 3(5)] and the emergency protection order should be sufficient to deal with any difficult situation which may occur.

Section 3(5) was not drafted with only local authorities in mind. It was suggested by the Law Commission as a general provision in child law; hence its appearance at the beginning of the Children Act. However, its wording might be thought to lend support to the Government's view. At this stage, though, we encounter a technical legal argument which may have the effect of undermining that view. The argument derives from the fact that section 3(5) is expressed to apply 'subject to the provisions of this Act' – in other words, it is subordinated to any other section or subsection which runs in the opposite direction. Section 20(8) is just such a provision, providing in the clearest possible terms for an unrestricted parental power to remove the child from accommodation. Consequently, the arguments based on section 3(5) may be unsound. Until the courts rule on the combined effect of section 20(8) and section 3(5), the legal position is unhappily obscure.

If the arguments based on section 3(5) do ultimately prevail, then 'unfit' parents may be kept at arm's length by the local authority. But while solving one problem, this creates others. For how long may the authority hold on to the child? Can the parents be kept away indefinitely? Can the authority retain the child on grounds unconnected with the parents' physical capacity to care, e.g. because a removal from accommodation would be emotionally upsetting for the child? It is a pity that the answers to important questions such as these remain unclear.

Help on leaving accommodation

The section 20 service is available for children right up to the age of 18. There is, in addition to the functions already described, a discretionary power to provide accommodation for those between 16 and 21 in any community home which takes children over 16, if the local authority considers that to do so would safeguard or promote their welfare. As we have seen, however, by the time they reach the age of 16, children acquire in effect the right to discharge themselves from care.

The acute problems of many of the children who leave local authority care were highlighted during the passage of the Children Act. Their problems could be said to fall into two broad categories, although they are certainly linked. The first problem is that of attracting emotional support from the social services department. The second concerns material support. Legislation aimed at

ensuring this support is not new: the Child Care Act 1980 contains
specific provisions on the subject. However, these were described as
'weak and confused', and consequently productive of wide variations in practice, by the House of Commons Social Services
Committee in its 1984 report, and this diagnosis was endorsed both
by the Review of Child Care Law and by the DoH in its White
Paper. The result of this dissatisfaction is a new set of provisions.
These are collected in section 24 of the Children Act.

Preparing for departure

The first of these provisions, section 24(1), is concerned not so much
with the child who has left accommodation, but with all children
currently being looked after by the local authority. It requires the
authority to advise, assist and befriend them with a view to
promoting their welfare when they cease to be looked after by it.
This may be regarded as a direct response to the problem identified
by the House of Commons Committee, whereby young people,
particularly those in community homes, are released from care with
insufficient preparation for life in the world outside. As the Review
of Child Care Law pointed out, however, this duty should not be
regarded as simply requiring the provision of an end-of-stay
package: 'the foundations for leaving care rest on the quality of the
young person's experience throughout his or her stay in care and on
the effectiveness of reviews'.

Needless to say, the nature of the preparatory work will vary
according to the characteristics of the child and the circumstances of
the case, e.g. whether he is returning to his family, or staying in his
present accommodation, or becoming fully independent and so on.
The 'assistance' which is given may be in kind or, in exceptional
circumstances, in cash (subject to the usual conditions, referred to
below).

Advice and assistance after departure

Section 24(2) is the new provision concerning those who have left
care. The 'target group' consists of persons under 21 who were
provided with section 20 accommodation at some time between the
ages of 16 and 18 but who are no longer so accommodated. Section
24 imposes a *duty* on the local authority to advise and befriend any
member of this group, provided certain conditions are fulfilled.
These are:

1   The authority knows he is in its area.
2   He has asked the authority for help.
3   It appears to the authority that he is in need of advice and
    being befriended.

In addition to the duty to advise and befriend, there is a discretionary *power* to give assistance. At this point, the section brings into play the usual rules governing the provision of 'assistance'. So that assistance given to the under-21s may be in kind, or in exceptional circumstances, in cash; it may be unconditional or subject to conditions as to repayment (in whole or in part); the means of the recipient must be taken into account; and no repayment can be demanded if he is receiving income support or family credit.

Several things need to be noted about these provisions. Firstly, their operation depends on the local authority acquiring knowledge that a person qualifying for help is in its area. Two further aspects of the Act should assist in this respect: section 24 requires every authority to inform another authority if a person they are advising under the section – and this would include those about to leave care – proposes to live in the area of that other authority; and Schedule 2 requires every authority to publish information about the services provided by it under section 24 and to take reasonable steps to ensure that those who might benefit from the services receive the information relevant to them.

Secondly, the duty only arises if a request is made. There is no question of thrusting advice, friendship and the rest down the throat of an unwilling recipient. Some children who are leaving, or who have left, local authority accommodation may not want help from that particular quarter. For the same reason, there is no legal obligation on the authority's part to track down members of the target group and offer help.

How exactly an authority responds to any request will obviously depend on the circumstances and, to a large extent, the judgment of the social worker. The nature of the response may also depend, heavily, on the state of the authority's budget. The provision of assistance, including cash in 'exceptional circumstances', to the under-21s on a discretionary basis gives rise to exactly the same problems as does its provision to children in need as part of a preventative strategy and to children being prepared for leaving care: different interpretations, leading to different policies based on different philosophies.

Accommodation and training

Section 24 empowers local authorities to give assistance to the persons described above by contributing to accommodation expenses incurred in connection with employment, education or training. It also empowers them to make grants to enable these persons to meet expenses connected with education and training.

Assistance with education and training can last beyond the age of 21.

Few would seek to argue that section 24 does not bring about a more coherent statutory framework for local authority involvement in after-care. Nor can it be denied that the voluntary sector makes an outstanding contribution in this field. But massive problems remain. Shortages of housing, employment and money will continue to afflict many of those leaving care, resulting in some cases in personal tragedy. Many would argue that this suffering is not unavoidable. Valiant attempts were made during the Parliamentary debates on the Children Act to strengthen the law in favour of care-leavers even further. Particular emphasis was given to the adverse effects of the new social security regime introduced during 1988. This, it was said, had a severe impact on young people living apart from their families; for children leaving care, the impact was especially hard. The Government resisted these attempts. Its argument was that the scope and purposes of the Act did not embrace alterations to housing law, social security law or any other branch of law which concerns the population generally, as opposed to children. Such an approach enabled the DoH to deflect the pressure for change onto other parts of the Government.

After-care for other children

This chapter is primarily concerned with those children provided with accommodation under section 20. Section 24 has been described with these in mind. It should be noted, however, that the provisions of section 24 also apply, with some variations, to care order children, children looked after in the private sector and children accommodated in certain health establishments.

The acquisition of control by the authority

Circumstances will arise, as they do at present, where the local authority feels that, in accordance with its general duty to safeguard and promote the child's welfare, it should acquire firm control over the future upbringing of the child. Although in providing accommodation under section 20 it will inevitably be intimately involved in the day-to-day care of the child, without more its power will be qualified, especially by the statutory right of the parents to remove the child from the accommodation. How may firm control be acquired?

It is a fundamental objective of the Children Act to bring about a situation whereby parental responsibility (i.e. parental rights) can only be acquired by a local authority through the medium of a court order. At the moment, authorities which have received a child into care are in a position to acquire 'the parental rights' through a resolution passed by the council under section 3 of the Child Care Act 1980. This machinery has been heavily criticised in recent years, in spite of its confirmation and expansion by the Children Act 1975, not so much because it has been misused by authorities but on grounds of principle. It has now been accepted, on virtually all sides, that to allow the State to deprive parents of their rights by an essentially administrative device is wrong. Accordingly, the parental rights resolution will become a thing of the past when the 1989 Act is implemented. To acquire compulsory powers, the local authority will have to go to court. This is an absolute rule: it applies whether the parents consent or not.

After the Children Act, there will be two ways, and only two ways, in which the local authority will be able to acquire long-term parental responsibility. The first is by obtaining a care order. The second is by obtaining, with the consent of a parent or guardian, an order under the Adoption Act 1976 freeing the child for adoption. In addition to these methods, short-term parental responsibility may be obtained through an emergency protection order. Such an order will often, of course, be a precursor to a care order. These three procedures are dealt with in later chapters.

It will be noticed that the acquisition of control via the wardship jurisdiction is not mentioned in the previous paragraph. This jurisdiction is available at present, and heavily used. However, as is explained in Chapter 15, the effect of the Children Act is to make it unavailable to local authorities in cases where they desire parental responsibility.

While the abolition of the parental rights resolution procedure will be widely welcomed as a matter of principle, difficulties in practice may arise out of restricting local authorities which want control to care and freeing-for-adoption proceedings. There may be cases where the authority wishes to get into a position in which it can take decisions in relation to a child whom it is accommodating but feels that a care order or a freeing order is either not obtainable or not desirable. It may, for example, wish to consent to important medical treatment or to some leisure activity, but feel that, not having parental responsibility, it cannot do so. If those who do have such responsibility, i.e. the parents, are not available or are not competent to consent, what is the authority to do?

Two solutions are offered by the Children Act. One is for the authority to apply to the court under section 8 for a specific issue order (described in Chapters 3 and 4). Getting directions from the court via such an order will clearly provide the necessary legal justification for taking the action in question. The second way out of any difficulty will be for the authority to go ahead with the action and, in the event of its legality being questioned, seek to rely on section 3(5) of the Act. As we saw earlier, this states that a person caring for a child may do what is reasonable in all the circumstances of the case for the purpose of safeguarding or promoting the child's welfare.

The acquisition of control by individuals

Just as the local authority can gain parental responsibility in respect of the accommodated child, so can individuals. Foster parents and relatives, for example, will have the opportunity of applying for a residence order under section 8 of the Act, in much the same way as they can now apply for custodianship. As was seen in Chapter 4, however, the Children Act draws a distinction between those non-parents who are entitled to seek a residence order and those who must first obtain the leave of the court. Moreover, in the case of foster parents, there may be a requirement to obtain the consent of the authority.

In addition to residence orders, adoption orders can be sought in respect of the accommodated child. Here, of course, the consent of the parents will need to be obtained, unless there are grounds for dispensing with it. Finally, it should not be forgotten that where the child has no parent with parental responsibility, the court may appoint an individual to be the child's guardian under section 5 of the Act (see Chapter 2).

7 Compulsory intervention: the new framework

Here is a simple, but important, question. What are the different ways in which public agencies, especially local authorities, can take action under statutory powers to acquire the exclusive right to care for a child, either temporarily or permanently? Consider in addition a supplementary question: once action has been taken, what is the precise legal position of (1) the agency; (2) the child; and (3) the child's family? How many of those working in the child care field know the answers to these questions? How easy is it to find out the answers by examining the statute book? In Chapter 1, attention was drawn to the scandalous state into which our public child law has been allowed to develop. This is one of the reasons why the answers to these last questions are all too obvious. As far as this branch of the law is concerned, the Children Act has two fundamental objectives:

1 To restate the rules relating to public agency intervention in clear and straightforward terms.
2 To give all the parties (and this includes the child) a fairer deal than they get at present.

The rules contained in the Children Act which are concerned with compulsory powers are to be found for the most part in Part I, Part IV and Part V. Schedule 3 acts as a supplement to Part IV. These rules establish the new framework for intervention. Many of them are quite detailed, but in some cases (needless to say) the Act leaves the detail to be supplied by government regulations. The features of the new framework are derived in the main from the Child Care Law Review of 1985 and the DoH White Paper of 1987. However, the 1988 Butler-Sloss report into child abuse in Cleveland and other ad hoc inquiry reports have also had some impact.

As has been said, it is one of the Act's principal objectives to restate the rules in a clear manner. What the Act does *not* do, however, is to tell public agencies when to use them; and in this respect it is no different from the existing legislation. It makes available to social workers, police officers and others a range of tools which are seen as appropriate and necessary for child protection work; it requires specified conditions to be fulfilled before action can be taken; it imposes procedural safeguards for the parties when action is taken; but it gives no orders about the employment of this machinery. The use of the new statutory procedures is a matter left to the judgement and discretion of the agency and those individuals working alongside it. There is no question of the statutory machinery having to be used in any given situation: the law's requirement is simply that the discretion is exercised in good faith, after a consideration of all the relevant factors. As the DoH put it recently, in the context of child abuse:

> Not all cases can or should come before the court. Each case is unique and it would be difficult to set out in detail factors that could influence this decision. In broad terms, the decision about court action is likely to be based on the nature of the abuse, the circumstances of the incident and the response of the parents, the initial assessment of parental ability to change, their acceptance of responsibility or acknowledgement of problems and their willingness to co-operate with the helping agencies (*Protecting Children: A Guide for Social Workers undertaking a Comprehensive Assessment* (1988)).

There is no objection to a particular agency, or a particular group or team within an agency, establishing a formal policy on the use of compulsory procedures. Experience has shown that such a device can produce positive benefits in terms of open, consistent and rational decision-making. But to remain within legal bounds, a policy must not be over-rigid; in other words, it must not preclude the examination of each case on its merits.

The tools given to agencies under the 1989 Act are five in number: the emergency protection order, the child assessment order, what I propose to call the police protection power, the care order and the supervision order. These five methods of compulsory intervention are described in the following chapters of this book, and in the order in which they have just been set out. This is not the order in which they appear in the Act but it may be thought appropriate to look at these methods in a temporal framework, recognising the fact that applications for care and supervision orders will often be preceded by the granting of the emergency and assessment orders.

The effect of this new regime will be to consign to history the compulsory power provisions of the Children and Young Persons Acts 1933 and 1969 and other existing statutes. In addition, the use of wardship by local authorities – of growing importance in recent years – will be severely restricted.

Inter-agency co-operation

> The problems of child sexual abuse have been recognised to an increasing extent over the past few years by professionals in different disciplines. This presents new and particularly difficult problems for the agencies concerned in child protection. In Cleveland an honest attempt was made to address these problems by the agencies. In Spring 1987 it went wrong. The reasons for the crisis are complex. In essence they included: lack of a proper understanding by the main agencies of each other's functions in relation to child sexual abuse; a lack of communication between the agencies ...

With a statement like that appearing at the forefront of the final conclusions of the Butler-Sloss report, it was inevitable that the need for effective inter-agency working would receive an even higher profile than normal in the period leading up to the Children Act. Of course, the exposure of poor relationships between different child care agencies is nothing new. It has been a depressingly prominent feature of numerous child-oriented inquiries and reports over the years. But the scale of the intervention which occurred in Cleveland, combined with the ensuing publicity, guaranteed that this issue would be highlighted. As with certain other aspects of child protection work, however, it is far easier to demonstrate past failings in co-operation than it is to construct a foolproof framework for the future. It is, moreover, particularly difficult to enshrine such a framework in law; this is partly because of the enormous variations in the types of case which can occur in practice and partly because of the differing ways in which the structures and traditions of agencies up and down the country have developed over the years.

The upshot of this difficulty is that co-operation between agencies has tended to be dealt with, not through the medium of legislation, but through the issue of guidance and advice. The Children Act does nothing to disturb this tradition. The farthest it goes is to authorise a local authority (not require, be it noted) to call upon other authorities to assist it while conducting enquiries with a view to possible action in support of a child. In the future, therefore, as in the past, local authorities and other institutions will have to be relied upon to abide by the spirit, if not the letter, of documents issued by the DoH and other co-ordinating bodies.

In this context, mention should be made of the publication entitled *Working Together*. This was issued by the Department in 1988 to coincide with the release of the Cleveland report. Its stated aim is to 'provide a guide to all the agencies involved in working together to protect children from abuse. It is essentially concerned with how agencies can develop agreed joint policies and the arrangements necessary for making them effective, both in respect of individual cases and in respect of the monitoring and review of practice and related management issues'. Of course, child care work, and therefore child care law, does not cover just child abuse. There are plenty of children's matters not touched upon in *Working Together*. But it is an important and recent example of the sort of official guidance which can be given to individuals in the field, with a view to achieving an effective multi-disciplinary approach. The document contains much detailed advice relating to the management of child abuse, and in particular sexual abuse cases, ranging from the holding of inter-agency case conferences and the designation of key workers to the operation of child protection registers and the formation of specialist assessment teams and Area Child Protection Committees. It is, in addition, careful to emphasise the various contributions which professionals, those in the voluntary sector and members of the general public can make to the successful handling of child abuse cases. Clearly, these are all important matters. None of them, however, is mentioned in the Children Act and anyone who takes a look at *Working Together*, or any other piece of official guidance, should quickly appreciate the impracticality of transforming its contents into fixed legal rules.

Those working with the new legislation should therefore understand that it needs to be read, not on its own, nor simply in conjunction with the many sets of government regulations which will be issued, but alongside all the relevant non-legal material as well. This may be confusing, but unfortunately it is unavoidable.

The investigation stage of intervention: the statutory duty of the local authority

Compulsory intervention under the Children Act can be directed towards children who are already being looked after by a local authority or other agency, as well as those presently living 'on the outside'. For those already in agency accommodation the investigation and assessment of the child's needs and general situation should take place as a matter of course, as part of the overall continuing welfare responsibility owed by the agency. Such assessment should obviously include a consideration of whether or not an application for compulsory powers is needed.

For children on the outside, whether living with their families or not, section 47 of the Children Act builds on the existing provisions in the Children and Young Persons Act 1969 and imposes a specific duty on the social services department to make, or cause to be made (i.e. arrange for others to do the job), 'such enquiries as they consider necessary to enable them to decide whether they should take any action to safeguard or promote the child's welfare'. This duty, which needless to say can be onerous and time-consuming, is triggered by the department having reasonable cause to suspect that a child who lives, or is found, in its area 'is suffering, or is likely to suffer, significant harm'. 'Harm' is a central concept in the compulsory power sections of the Children Act and, as will be seen in Chapter 10, is defined expansively so as to cover ill-treatment or the impairment of health or development. Whether or not there is reasonable cause to suspect significant harm is wholly dependent upon the particular circumstances. It is a matter for professional judgement. There is, however, a provision buried at the back of the Act which should not be overlooked in this context. Schedule 2, which is devoted to local authority support for children (see Chapter 5), states that where a local authority believes that a child within its area is likely to suffer harm but lives or proposes to live in the area of another authority, that other authority must be informed of the details. Where this information is transmitted, the receiving authority will probably feel that section 47 should be put into effect.

The local authority's duty, then, is to make enquiries to enable it to decide whether it should take any action. 'Action', for these purposes, can embrace many things, of course, and may simply involve the provision of advice and information (not necessarily by the authority) to the child and/or his carers. At the other end of the spectrum, there is the compulsory intervention machinery, and this is expressly mentioned in section 47: 'the enquiries shall, in particular, be directed towards establishing whether the authority should make any application to the court'. If, on the conclusion of the enquiries, the authority decides not to apply for an emergency protection order, a child assessment order, a care order, or a supervision order, it must consider whether it would be appropriate to review the case at a later date and if it decides that this would be appropriate, it must fix a date for that review.

As previously mentioned, the Act empowers the local authority to call upon others to assist it during the enquiry process. These others are: any other local authority, any local education authority, any local housing authority, any health authority, and any person specified by government regulations for the purposes of the section. They must all assist the investigating department unless this would be unreasonable in all the circumstances. The list of consultees is obviously not exhaustive. The police and the probation service, for example, are only missing from the list for technical reasons. Where the child is ordinarily resident in the area of another local authority, that other authority must be consulted; and where it emerges that there are matters connected with the child's education which should be investigated, the LEA must be consulted.

Apart from the duty to see the child, discussed below, this is as far as the Act goes in terms of directing the course of an investigation. But the Act is only part of the picture: nationally agreed guidelines, such as those contained in *Working Together* and *Protecting Children*, and locally agreed procedures, need to be borne in mind at all times, because it is likely that very detailed 'rules' concerning investigations will be set out in them. This is certainly true of *Working Together*, which discusses the investigatory functions not just of the social services department, but also of the NSPCC and the police, and emphasises the need for enquiries to be pursued on a multi-agency, multi-disciplinary basis.

Seeing the child

This has become a crucial matter. According to *Working Together*, the initial steps for an investigatory agency must be to 'establish the relevant factual circumstances of the child and the possible sources of harm or danger'. The refusal of the child's carer to allow agency representatives to see the child, which will almost certainly have the effect of blocking the investigation, was an eventuality which was bound to generate discussion in the context of the Children Act. One of the reasons for this was the publicity given to the Kimberley Carlile case and the ensuing inquiry report compiled by Louis Blom-Cooper and others (*A Child in Mind* (1987)). This case contained many different strands of child care issues but it is likely to be remembered as the one in which the social worker carrying out a visit to the family home was only permitted to view the child through a small glass panel in a door. The breaking of the Doreen Mason case in December 1988, shortly after the introduction of the Children Bill, only served to highlight the importance of the access issue, because there too social workers were obstructed.

A direct result of this concern is that, in contrast to the existing legislation, there are specific references to access in the Children Act. Some of them relate to emergency protection orders and child assessment orders – indeed, the child assessment order largely owes its existence to the issue. The relevant provisions are discussed in subsequent chapters, but for the moment, it will be sufficient to mention what section 47 of the Act has to say about the denial of access and information during a local authority investigation.

The section states first of all that where enquiries are being made, the local authority shall take such steps as are reasonably practicable to obtain access to the child or to ensure that access to him is obtained on its behalf by an authorised person, unless it is satisfied that it already has sufficient information about him. So there is a statutory assumption that the child will be visited by, or on behalf of, the social services department. If the child's carer is obstructive, another provision within section 47 comes into play: where any local authority officer or authorised person is refused access to the child or is denied information as to his whereabouts, the authority shall apply for an emergency protection order, a child assessment order, a care order or a supervision order unless it is satisfied that his welfare can be satisfactorily safeguarded without its doing so.

This latter provision is the nearest the Act comes to telling a local authority when to embark on compulsory intervention procedures. While it is framed as a duty, there are two important discretionary elements. First, proceedings will not need to be taken if the local authority is satisfied that the welfare proviso at the end is satisfied. For example, it may be that action to be taken by the police will be regarded as a sufficient response to the problem, at least for the time being. Second, even if proceedings are to be taken, the local authority has a choice as to which form of compulsory order to go for. The combination of these two qualifications does obviously give the investigating team considerable room for manoeuvre. At the same time, however, the wording of the provision remains strong and reflects the view of the Government and others that the frustration of a local authority child abuse investigation is a matter to be taken extremely seriously. As the Minister of Health put it: 'We do not want people to be able to say, "I have not seen the child for myself, the wounds have not been exposed and therefore there is no reason for action".'

Questions may arise as to the meaning of 'access' in this context. Suppose the social worker is asked to stay on the doorstep while the child is brought to the top of the stairs. Is access being granted or denied? Many other scenarios can be easily envisaged. It is suggested that 'access', interpreted in the light of the purposes of the Act and its background, must mean face-to-face contact which lasts for a reasonable time. If the child's carer does not satisfy the investigating team on this score, it may be felt appropriate to warn him of the effect of the Act and the possible consequences of his intransigence.

Examination and assessment of the child

Gaining access to the child in an investigation is vital. But what about the allied matter of medical and similar examinations? Can the child's carer be instructed by the investigating team to present the child to a health service professional? Here too, the public has been made aware by events such as the Carlile case of the difficulties, practical and legal, caused by obdurate families. The effect of the Children Act will be to make available a wider range of compulsory measures in the event of a total and unreasonable refusal by the carer to co-operate. Social workers are not given the power to carry out forcibly an examination themselves, nor have they the power to order an examination; but they are given the power to seek such an order from the court. This can be done either as part of an emergency protection order, or under a child assessment order, both of which are discussed in the following chapter. Having such remedies available should enable the investigators to exert considerable pressure on the carer. After all, there is little difference in purely practical terms between a social worker making and then serving a medical examination order on a person, and giving him a letter stating that an emergency protection order or child assessment order will be sought if the child is not presented to a doctor within 24 hours.

8 Emergency protection orders and child assessment orders

Introduction

This chapter is devoted to two completely separate types of court order. This may seem a strange sort of arrangement but the connections between the two orders are such as to make it appropriate to treat them together. We enter an area of considerable controversy at this stage, because whereas the need for an emergency protection order (EPO) has never been doubted by those involved in the present reform of children's law, the child assessment order (CAO) is entering life without a universal blessing. Significantly, perhaps, the CAO was not part of the package recommended by the Review of Child Care Law in 1985; nor was it endorsed in the Government's 1987 White Paper. It was mentioned in the 1988 Butler-Sloss report into the Cleveland affair but the inquiry came out firmly against it. And it did not appear in the Children Bill when the Bill was first presented to Parliament. It is therefore hardly surprising that its eventual emergence in the Act has been troubled.

The EPO and the CAO have various things in common. Both are forms of compulsory intervention aimed at protecting children. Both are available only through the court system. Both are short-term measures, which may or may not lead to an application for a care order or a supervision order. Note the contrasting features, however. The EPO will be available from a single magistrate, whereas the CAO will only be obtainable from a full court. The EPO will be available on an 'ex parte' basis, i.e. without a hearing at which the parents are able to be present. The CAO can only be made after a full hearing (inter partes, in legal terms, as opposed to ex parte). It is not, therefore, aimed at emergencies. Most importantly, the EPO will authorise the removal of the child from his carer into any suitable accommodation. The CAO will not normally go this far. For this reason, the CAO is undoubtedly the lesser order. The new challenge for child protection professionals is to recognise when to use, and when not to use, each one.

The emergency protection order

The discredited place of safety order

The EPO is designed to replace the place of safety order. Under the existing law, there are at least five separate statutory procedures whereby a place of safety order may be made, the most well-known being the one created by section 28 of the Children and Young Persons Act 1969. All these procedures are swept away by the Children Act.

The place of safety order has been the subject of a number of criticisms in recent years. Its name is said to conceal the fact that it is, or should be, only aimed at emergencies; it can last for 28 days, an excessively long period; the legal position of the various parties during the place of safety period is unclear; and there is no effective right of challenge available to the child's family. These faults are all contained in the legislation and can therefore be corrected fairly easily. What is perhaps more difficult to adjust is the way in which the legislation is actually used in the field. Here too, there have been criticisms, not least in relation to the events in Cleveland during 1987: the place of safety order positively dominates the 300-page report compiled by Dame Elizabeth Butler-Sloss. This searching examination of child protection practices in one small part of the country guaranteed the order and its successor the very highest of profiles during the passage of the Children Act.

The range of applicants for an EPO

Anybody can apply for a place of safety order under the existing Children and Young Persons Act and the Children Act does nothing to change the position: section 44 refers to an application made by 'any person'. So that social workers, police officers, health visitors, teachers and other professionals will continue to have ready access to the courts.

It should be noted that section 52 of the Act enables regulations to be made by the Government providing for a transfer of responsibilities under an EPO to the local authority within whose area the child is ordinarily resident. This will, of course, only be relevant in those cases where the applicant for the order was not that authority. If such a transfer does take place (and it will be a matter for the authority's discretion), the authority will be treated as though it had applied for the order: so it will acquire decision-making power (and duties) in the case and the original applicant will lose it.

The grounds for an EPO

The grounds for an EPO are set out in section 44. According to this, the court may make an order if, but only if, it is satisfied that:

(a) there is reasonable cause to believe that the child is likely to suffer significant harm if (i) he is not removed to accommodation provided by or on behalf of the applicant; or (ii) he does not remain in the place in which he is then being accommodated;

(b) in the case of an application made by a local authority (i) enquiries are being made under section 47 and (ii) those enquiries are being frustrated by access to the child being unreasonably refused to a person authorised to seek access and the authority has reasonable cause to believe that access to the child is required as a matter of urgency; or

(c) in the case of an application made by the NSPCC (i) it has reasonable cause to suspect that a child is suffering, or is likely to suffer, significant harm; (ii) it is making enquiries with respect to the child's welfare; and (iii) those enquiries are being frustrated etc. (as in (b)).

The section makes it clear that 'a person authorised to seek access' means an officer of the local authority or someone authorised by the authority to act on its behalf, or the NSPCC.

As can be seen, the Act sets out three distinct grounds for an EPO. When it was first presented to Parliament, the Children Bill only contained ground (a). Grounds (b) and (c), which are concerned with the blocking of official child protection enquiries through the denial of access to the child, are a reflection of the great importance which the DoH now attaches to this particular issue. We have seen in Chapter 7 how section 47 of the Act virtually directs a local authority to seek compulsory powers where access is refused to an investigating team; and we shall see later in the present chapter how the issue of access has played a part in the creation of the child assessment order. This need to see the child has become one of the clearest messages which the Act is sending out to social workers.

Several points concerning the interpretation of section 44 need mentioning here. As far as paragraph (a) is concerned, its forward-looking wording is a distinct improvement on the existing section 28 of the Children and Young Persons Act 1969, as is its express reference to the situation where the child needs to stay put (as opposed to being removed). The expression 'significant harm' is a crucial one and occurs in several places in the Act. Its meaning is discussed in Chapter 10 (see page 108).

With regard to paragraphs (b) and (c), the reason for their appearance in the Act has already been explained. While anybody may apply for an EPO under paragraph (a), paragraphs (b) and (c) are reserved for the use of social services departments and the NSPCC. It will be noticed that paragraph (c) refers to the NSPCC having reasonable cause to suspect significant harm, while paragraph (b) does not mention harm. The difference is more apparent than real, however, because the local authority enquiries referred to in (b) are themselves conditioned on a reasonable suspicion of harm (see Chapter 7).

'Access' is not defined in the Act but as stated in Chapter 7, it is suggested that it involves face-to-face contact with the child which lasts for a reasonable time. It would seem that the contact does not need to be in the child's home.

Grounds (b) and (c) refer to access being 'unreasonably refused'. Whether or not this condition is satisfied is ultimately a question of fact for the court or magistrate to decide. Social workers should obviously be aware of the need to explain their position in calm and clear terms to the child's carer and to produce official identification if requested. If their request to see the child is mismanaged, his carer might be fully justified in adopting a negative approach.

The court's discretion

As with the other types of compulsory intervention, the court is not obliged to grant an application for an EPO. The court, or magistrate, guided by the welfare principle set out in section 1 of the Act, will need to consider carefully whether the order is available (i.e. have grounds been made out) and whether making it would be better for the child than making no order at all. Needless to say, this should not be a mere rubber-stamping exercise (a point hammered home in the aftermath of the Cleveland affair). Concern has been expressed in recent years about the use of place of safety orders in non-emergency situations and the hope is that social workers and the courts will be aware of the dangers of such a practice. As the Review of Child Care Law commented: 'An EPO should not become a matter of course where care proceedings are a likely option.'

The checklist of factors set out in section 1 of the Act (discussed in Chapter 3) does not strictly speaking apply to EPO applications, on account of the urgency of the cases, but no doubt elements of it will be used in practice.

The legal effect of an EPO

As previously explained, the precise legal consequences of a place of safety order are unclear. The EPO provisions of the Children Act address this question directly.

The first legal consequence is that the order operates as a direction to any person who is in a position to do so to comply with any request to produce the child to the applicant. Disobedience of this deemed direction can be punished as a contempt of court and those who know where the child is should obviously be made aware of this if they prove obstructive.

The second, and critical, consequence is that the applicant may lawfully remove the child from his present residence to other accommodation *or* prevent his removal from his present residence (e.g. a hospital or a foster home). Anyone who intentionally obstructs the exercise of this power commits a criminal offence. An important feature of this provision is that it gives the applicant a discretion: in other words, the applicant does not have to exercise the power to remove or detain. Indeed, section 44 states that the power shall only be exercised 'in order to safeguard the welfare of the child'. This flexibility is essential if social workers and other professionals are to respond to what are often rapidly-changing circumstances. An obvious example is where a suspected abuser leaves the family home between the time of the application for the order and the time when the social worker arrives at the doorstep. Another is where the suspected abuser is prepared to give an undertaking to leave the home. On this point, it is worth noting that Schedule 2 of the Act enables a local authority to assist such persons in obtaining alternative accommodation. This can include the provision of cash (subject to the usual conditions as to repayment). Clearly, the exercise of this power, in preference to the removal of the child, will need to be accompanied by extreme care and consideration.

Similarly, there is discretion to backtrack once the power has been used: if it appears to the applicant that it is safe for the child to be returned, that action should, under section 44, be taken. By the same token, however, if circumstances again change while the order is in force, the power to remove can be reactivated. The child's carers (or would-be carers) should obviously be told at the outset, and in clear terms, how the making of an EPO gives the applicant full power to determine the child's place of residence for the duration of the order.

Many children removed under EPOs will be placed in local authority accommodation. Where this occurs, the child is within the category of those being 'looked after'. The significance of this is that the code of treatment set out in Part III of the Act becomes applicable (except for the parental contribution rules). This code is described in Chapter 6.

The third legal consequence of an EPO is that it gives the applicant parental responsibility (i.e. parental powers and duties) in respect of the child. Doing this does not deprive the parents of their parental responsibility – as we saw in Chapter 2, only adoption will have this effect – but it does give the holder of the EPO legal authority to take decisions concerning the child while he is under protection. However, we are dealing here with a short-term measure; for the holder to take a decision with long-term implications for the child would clearly be inappropriate. The Children Act attempts to cover this point by stating (section 44(5)) that the holder 'shall take and shall only take such action as is reasonably required to safeguard or promote the welfare of the child (having regard in particular to the duration of the order)'. This is a trifle vague, of course, and it may lead to variations in practice, but given the variety of situations encountered it is probably the best that can be achieved in a statute. Perhaps greater precision will be produced by the supplementary regulations which the DoH will make in this area: it is possible that certain types of decision will only be available to the holder in restricted circumstances.

Two specific aspects of parental responsibility are dealt with by special provisions: contact and medical examinations. These matters, which caused great problems in the Cleveland affair, are discussed in the following sections.

Contact

The effect of the Act is to clarify and improve the position of parents and others connected with the child, following the exercise of emergency protection powers. The provisions are modelled on those pertaining to care orders, so there is a statutory presumption in favour of contact. The applicant (e.g. the local authority) is to allow the child 'reasonable contact' with: the parents (this includes the unmarried father), non-parents with parental responsibility, anybody living with the child prior to the order, anybody holding a contact order, and anybody acting on behalf of these people. There is no indication in the Act as to what is reasonable.

Should the applicant wish to restrict contact or stop it completely (and obviously there will be many such cases), the court can be asked to give appropriate directions, either at the time the EPO is made or subsequently. Conversely, the court can at any stage issue directions, with conditions attached, if necessary, in favour of contact with any person. This facility may be of help to those family members who are unhappy with the amount of contact being offered by the holder of the EPO. Any direction as to contact can be varied subsequently.

These provisions on contact are not the only ones which need to be borne in mind. As was explained earlier, if an EPO child is removed into local authority accommodation, he becomes subject to the code of treatment set out in Part III of the Act. This code contains contact rules too (see Chapter 6); it also deals with local authority complaints procedures and these will cover EPO children.

Medical examination and assessment

Commenting on the uncertainties surrounding the existing place of safety order legislation, the Cleveland inquiry team said:

> We would suggest that an initial examination to ascertain the health of a child would be within the authorisation of the agency under the order, and in a case such as physical injury, X-rays and any consequential necessary treatment would follow. It would not however in our view include repeat examinations for forensic purposes or for information gathering rather than for continuing treatment. Such examinations would require the consent of the parents. A situation might well arise and indeed did arise in Cleveland where there were excessive numbers of medical examinations of certain children. Some control over examinations in the present climate is now highly desirable ...

The Children Act introduces such control. Section 44 states that where the court makes an EPO it can give such directions (if any) as it considers appropriate with respect to the medical or psychiatric examination or other assessment of the child. Such a direction may be to the effect that there is to be no examination or assessment, or none without the court's consent. Furthermore, a direction can be given at any time while the EPO is in force and can be varied by the court. Finally, when making an EPO, the court can direct that the applicant, when exercising any powers, be accompanied by a doctor, nurse or health visitor.

A very important qualification of the above rule is contained in section 44: the child may refuse to submit to an examination or an assessment if he is of sufficient understanding to make an informed decision. The same rule is to be found in the provisions relating to interim orders and child assessment orders. It represents a victory for those who champion the rights of children and their right to be treated wherever possible in the same way as adults, and it has prevailed over the argument that in some cases the child's 'refusal' is not completely genuine but a product of parental pressure.

Many doctors can be expected to err on the side of caution in applying the provision just described. This is particularly so in view of a comment made in Parliament by the Minister of Health. He said that 'even if it were deemed that [he] was not a child with full understanding of the process, I do not believe that any medical practitioner would carry out a medical examination if a child resisted it. I believe that that would be in line with what we know about medical ethics.' In such cases, it becomes a matter of persuading the child, rather than compelling him.

The procedural aspects of EPOs

The Children Act is virtually silent on this matter, leaving it to be regulated by government rules. Aspects which will certainly feature in the rules are the extent to which EPO applications can be handled by a single magistrate, as opposed to a full court, and the extent to which parents and others will have to be notified of the order. Another aspect is the appointment of guardians ad litem. As we will see in Chapter 14, the Act does provide for the introduction of GALs into EPO proceedings, but the precise mechanics of this innovation, which has the potential for causing many practical problems, remain unclear.

The duration of an EPO

'An emergency protection order shall have effect for such period, not exceeding eight days, as may be specified in the order.' This is what section 45 provides. If the last of the eight days is a Sunday, or a bank holiday, or Good Friday or Christmas Day, the court can specify a period which ends at noon on the first later day which is not such a holiday. And if the EPO is made following the exercise of the police protection power (see Chapter 9) time starts to run from the first day of that period.

One extension of an EPO is possible, on application by a social services department or the NSPCC. This can last for up to seven days. However, it is only available where the court has reasonable cause to believe that the child is likely to suffer significant harm if the order is not extended.

These rules will inevitably have the effect of putting social workers and their legal advisers under more pressure, in terms of looking ahead and preparing a case, than the existing 28 day provisions do.

The parents' right of challenge

The Act paves the way for a long-awaited development: the introduction of an effective right for parents and others to challenge emergency removal of children. The challenge will be by way of an application to the court to discharge the EPO and section 45 makes it available to the parents, non-parents with parental responsibility, any person living with the child prior to the order, and the child himself.

The catch is that a challenge cannot be made (i.e. heard by the court) until 72 hours have expired. This mandatory period of delay is considered necessary so as to enable the holder of the order to assemble a case. Nor will a challenge be possible if the aggrieved party was given notice of, and was present at, the hearing at which the EPO was made – only one right of reply is available. And there is no right to challenge an EPO which has been extended, because the parties will have had an opportunity to question the extension when it was ordered.

What if the EPO is refused?

There is no right of appeal against a refusal of an EPO. The unsuccessful applicant may be able to institute wardship proceedings as a way round this, except for local authorities, whose use of wardship is heavily circumscribed by the Act (see Chapter 15). Alternatively, the police can be asked to intervene under their protection power. This will only have a limited duration, however.

Supplementary powers: locating the child

Section 48 of the Act contains provisions aimed at the effective enforcement of EPOs.

- Where it appears to the court that adequate information as to the child's whereabouts is not available to the applicant but is available to another person, it may include in the EPO a provision requiring that other person to disclose, on request, what he knows. Disobedience of such a requirement can be punished as a contempt of court.
- An EPO can authorise the applicant to enter specified premises and search for the child. Anyone intentionally obstructing the applicant commits a criminal offence.
- An EPO authorising an entry and search may also authorise a search for other children believed to be on the premises. In these circumstances, the applicant may, if the other children are found, proceed as if an EPO had been made in respect of them too, provided he or she is satisfied that the statutory grounds exist. The court must be notified of what happens.
- The police can be brought in to assist in the exercise of EPO powers. This matter is dealt with in Chapter 9.

The consequences of an EPO

There are, obviously, numerous possible consequences of EPO powers being used. It may be that an application for an interim order will follow; it may be that the child will be allowed to return home free of the threat of further intervention. It should be noted, however, that the making of an EPO must lead to an investigation by the local authority, whether or not it was the applicant for the order. This is required by section 47 of the Act, whose provisions are discussed in Chapter 7.

The child assessment order

The rationale of the CAO was explained by the Government to the House of Commons in the following way:

> The difficulty is to know whether the emergency protection order is adequate or whether we require an additional order – a child assessment order – to run in parallel with it. There may be a repeated failure to produce a child and perhaps it cannot be asserted that the matter is quite so urgent that there is an immediate need to intervene to take the child away – it is at the heart of our concerns that the emergency protection order is used only in those very serious circumstances, so the issue is whether there should be a lesser order requiring the production of a child and one which allows for the assessment of the child to take place. Section 43 represents the best attempt that the Government can make to take on board the various views and produce an easy-to-use, readily explicable proposition, which has the proper safeguards that one would expect when any intrusion into the rights of parents over their children is considered.

The range of applicants for a CAO

Whereas anybody may apply for an EPO, only local authorities and the NSPCC can apply for a CAO.

Grounds for a CAO

The court may make an order if, but only if, it is satisfied that:

(a)   the applicant has reasonable cause to suspect that the child is suffering, or is likely to suffer, significant harm; *and*

(b)   an assessment of the state of the child's health or development, or of the way in which he has been treated, is required to enable the applicant to determine whether or not the child is suffering, or is likely to suffer, significant harm; *and*

(c)   it is unlikely that such an assessment will be made, or be satisfactory, in the absence of an order.

It will be noticed that the first condition is based on the applicant having reasonable cause to suspect. This may be contrasted with other conditions in the Act which refer to the applicant having reasonable cause to believe, e.g. in relation to EPOs. As for the third condition, the Government's view is that 'the court is likely to be prepared to give an order only when it is clear that all reasonable attempts have been made to secure voluntary co-operation. Procedural rules will require the applicant to explain what steps he has taken to secure an assessment of the child.'

The legal effect of a CAO

The sole purpose of a CAO is to bring about an assessment of the child. As was noted in Chapter 7, assessment is not the same thing as a social worker obtaining access to a child. It is symptomatic of the confusion which has surrounded the CAO that some of its supporters have seen it as a way of responding to denials of access. The Government met this concern by widening the grounds for an EPO, but it insisted that the CAO still had a place in the Act.

According to section 43(5), a CAO must specify the date by which the assessment is to begin and shall have effect for such period, not exceeding seven days beginning with that date, as may be specified in the order.

Section 43(6) states that it shall be the duty of 'any person who is in a position to produce the child' (this does not simply mean the parents, of course) to produce him to such person as may be named in the order and to comply with such directions relating to assessment as the court thinks fit to specify.

Section 43(7) expressly authorises the assessment professional(s) to undertake the assessment in accordance with the terms of the order. This means that no parental consent will be needed, provided, of course, that the assessment does not go beyond the proper boundaries. Doctors and other members of the assessment team will need to take great care in adhering to the task described in the court's order.

Section 43(8) is an important, Gillick-inspired, provision. It enables a child who is of sufficient understanding to make an informed decision to refuse to submit to a medical or psychiatric examination or other assessment. Those engaged in assessment will need to think long and hard before proceeding with a protesting child, even if there is a feeling that the seeds of the opposition have been planted by a suspected abuser.

Separation of the child and his family

Supporters of the CAO have always gone out of their way to emphasise how different it would be from an EPO, and in particular, how the CAO would not involve the removal of the child from his family. 'Its prime virtue,' said the Kimberley Carlile inquiry team, 'would be that it would partake of none of the coercive nature of a removal and detention of a child from the child's parents and home ... since the order would not physically order the detachment of the child from its parents, there should be no question of family trauma.' Things have not turned out quite like this. A CAO may well involve the separation of the child from his family, because not all assessments can be carried out at a doctor's surgery or a clinic: residence in a hospital may be necessary if a thorough assessment is to be undertaken. This sort of scenario is explicitly mentioned in the Children Act. Section 43(9) states that:

> The child may only be kept away from home – (a) in accordance with directions specified in the order; (b) if necessary for the purposes of the assessment; and (c) for such period or periods as may be specified in the order.

The period specified cannot exceed seven days, of course, since that is the maximum duration of a CAO. And the specifying will be done by the court, not the social workers. The inevitable result, however, is that there will be cases where the court orders the removal of a child into a health service establishment for a week. The parents will not lose parental responsibility but they will lose the child. In these circumstances, the differences between a CAO and an EPO may be difficult for them to appreciate. No question of family trauma?

A concession to family unity is made by section 43(10), which requires the court, where the child is to be kept away from home, to make such directions as it thinks fit with regard to the contact that the child must be allowed to have with other persons while away.

Defiance of a CAO

The CAO will require the child's present carer to 'produce' him to a named person. The court's supplementary directions must also be complied with. Suppose the carer fails to co-operate? There are several possible responses to this:

- The authorities could choose to do nothing. This might apply if their fears about the child prove to be unfounded before the assessment is actually carried out.

- The carer could be threatened with sanctions for contempt of court.

- The authorities could apply, or threaten to apply, for an EPO. Such an order would give them the power forcibly to remove the child.

Action following the assessment

Again, there are many possible outcomes of an assessment. What ultimately happens will depend on two factors in particular: the conclusions of the assessment professional(s) and the degree of co-operation which can be expected from the child's carer. These factors will dictate what sort of action, if any, is needed. Further compulsory intervention may be high on the agenda (an outcome which the carer will have been acutely aware of from the beginning).

One problem area has been highlighted by critics of the CAO: what can be done to protect the child immediately, if it becomes apparent during the assessment that abuse has been taking place? Obviously an EPO can be sought, but that takes time. An alternative strategy is to summon the police and invite them to exercise their protection power (on which see Chapter 9). That apart, it has to be said that without clear statutory authority to detain the child, doctors and social workers are in a precarious legal position. It is worth remembering, however, that this is the case when abuse is detected during a 'voluntary' examination.

Procedure

The CAO machinery is not aimed at emergencies and this is reflected in the procedural provisions. Under section 43(11), any person applying for a CAO shall take such steps as are reasonably practicable to ensure that notice of the application is given to various parties. These are: the child's parents, any non-parent having parental responsibility, any other person with whom the child is living, any person holding a contact order, and the child himself.

The precise form of the court hearing will be laid down by government rules, although it appears that a GAL will usually be appointed to represent the child.

Variation and discharge

CAOs will be amenable to variation and revocation but the Children Act does not specify the details. Section 43 leaves them to be spelled out by government rules.

Limits on the number of applications

Under section 91 of the Act, once a CAO application has been made, no further application can be made for six months without the leave of the court. This should be seen as an attempt to prevent the CAO being used oppressively.

CAO or EPO?

Ever since the CAO was first mooted, it has been recognised that its creation would throw up dilemmas for child protection workers. One of the main fears has been that social workers would, in an attempt to cause minimum damage to the family, go for the softer option, the CAO, and thereby do a disservice to the child who is in need of immediate removal from his home. The Kimberley Carlile inquiry team expressed this very clearly:

> The only worry that we entertain is whether there might not be a kind of bureaucratic magnetism about the lesser order. What we fear might happen is that social workers would too readily opt for the child assessment order in circumstances where their clear duty would be to apply for an emergency protection order. This real danger can be countered by social services directorates issuing clear instructions about the proper use of the two discrete orders. So long as social workers understand the different functions, there ought not to be any confusion about their use.

Opinions differ as to whether this view was over-optimistic. Certainly the Act contains no explicit guidance on how the choice between CAO and EPO (which, as we have seen, can itself contain directions for medical assessment) is to be made. However, what the Act does do – ominously, perhaps – is to acknowledge that applications for the wrong order will be made, because section 43 enables the court to treat an application for a CAO as an application for an EPO. It goes on to say that the court shall not make a CAO if it is satisfied that there are grounds for making an EPO and that it ought to make such an order rather than a CAO. Accordingly, social workers applying for CAOs may expect to be questioned very closely in court to see whether they have fallen victims to the bureaucratic magnetism described in the Carlile report.

There is another dimension to the dilemma, however. The Carlile inquiry envisaged the CAO as an order obtainable from a single magistrate without notice being given to the child's carer. That is not how things have turned out: as we have seen, a CAO will only be available on an 'inter partes' basis. From the social worker's point of view, applying to a single magistrate – which of course will be possible in the case of an EPO – may appear far more convenient and effective than having to go through a full hearing, with all the delays and complications which that can entail. The inter partes aspect of the CAO may indeed prove to be its Achilles heel. A more attractive option may be to go straight for an EPO, or else to warn the child's carer, formally or informally, that if the child is not brought for an assessment by a certain date, an EPO will be sought. This last device, which is quite lawful, comes very close to the issue of a 'child production notice' which has found favour with some critics.

It takes no great imagination to see the practical problems which will arise out of the CAO provisions of the Children Act, well-intentioned as they are. Unlike the other compulsory intervention provisions, they are not the product of the painstaking review of public child law which has been carried out in the last five years, but are a last-minute compromise between the views of various interest groups (notably the ADSS and the NSPCC). Considerable variations in their use can be expected. So can considerable confusion (it is, perhaps, significant that when examples were given in Parliament of situations where a CAO would fit the bill, others responded that in such circumstances the correct course would be to apply for an EPO).

9   Police powers

Police involvement in child protection cases tends to be transient and sporadic but it is nonetheless important. Like the existing child care legislation, the Children Act contains specific provisions relating to the police. These fall naturally into two categories: those which concern action taken on the initiative of the police, and those which concern the role of the police in assisting others.

The power of the police to act of their own motion

The lead provision here is section 46. This enables a constable (which in law means any police officer) simply to remove a child to suitable accommodation and keep him there; alternatively, a constable can take such steps as are reasonable to prevent the child's removal from his current accommodation (a removal from hospital is the obvious example of the sort of situation which Parliament has in mind here and section 46 mentions this expressly). Once such action is taken, the child is said to be in 'police protection', and he can be kept there for up to 72 hours.

It should be noted that the power given by this section is a power to remove or detain. This is quite distinct from a power to enter property, on which the section is silent. If a police officer wishes to exercise his power of protection but the child is on private property, he will have to look to some other provision for authority to enter the premises where the child is residing. In this connection, it is worth bearing in mind section 17 of the Police and Criminal Evidence Act 1984, for this permits a constable to enter and search any premises without a search warrant if his purpose is to save life or limb.

Clearly, the power to intervene under section 46 is a drastic one. It is not particularly novel, however, since a similar power may be found in the Children and Young Persons Act 1969, although following the Review of Child Care Law the opportunity has been taken to revise the rules. The police protection power will only be available where a constable has reasonable cause to believe that the child would otherwise be likely to suffer significant harm. The expression 'significant harm' takes us on to the new grounds laid down by the Children Act for a care order, and in fact it bears the same meaning as it does in section 31 (on which see page 108).

What happens once the child is taken into police protection obviously depends on the circumstances, but whatever the situation, certain rules have to be complied with as soon as is reasonably practicable:

- The constable must inform the local social services department of the steps which have been (and are proposed to be) taken with respect to the child and the reasons for taking them.
- The constable must notify the social services department for the child's home area of his current place of residence (a statutory acknowledgement that the protection power will be used on runaway children).
- If he appears capable of understanding, the child must be informed of the steps which have been taken with respect to him and the reasons for taking them, as well as the further steps which may be taken.
- The constable must take such steps as are reasonably practicable to discover the wishes and feelings of the child.
- The case must be inquired into by an officer designated for the purpose by the Chief Constable.
- If the child has initially been taken to accommodation which is not local authority accommodation or an approved refuge (on this, see Chapter 20), he must be moved to such a place.
- Certain persons must be informed of what has happened and why, and of what may happen. These are: the child's parents, any non-parent with parental responsibility, and any other person with whom the child was living immediately before being taken into protection. This duty links in with the family contact provisions noted below.

The position of the designated officer

It can be seen that once the police protection power is used, attention shifts to the designated officer and to the local social services department. As far as the former is concerned, he must carry out an inquiry into the case. Section 46(5) states that on completing this, he is to release the child unless he considers that there is still reasonable cause for believing that the child would be likely to suffer significant harm if released. If he decides to retain the child, the section permits him to apply, on behalf of the social services department for the child's home area, for an emergency protection order. In this way, continuity of care can be ensured. In the meantime, the designated officer, while not having parental responsibility, is empowered – indeed, obliged – to do what is reasonable in all the circumstances for the purpose of safeguarding or promoting the child's welfare. The Act does not envisage any long-term decisions being taken.

Family contact during the police protection period is regulated by section 46(10). The designated officer is to allow five categories of individual such contact (if any) with the child as, in his opinion, is both reasonable and in the child's best interests. These categories are: the parents, any non-parent with parental responsibility, any person who was living with the child before the police action, any person holding a contact order, and any person acting on behalf of these persons.

The position of the social services department

What is the position of the SSD? If the above-mentioned rules are followed, the child may find himself at an early stage in departmental accommodation (unless of course the police protection consists of preventing, rather than effecting, the removal of the child). The Children Act requires every local authority to make provision for the reception and maintenance of children in the category now under consideration. Once in such accommodation, the child falls within the provisions of Part III of the Act concerning children being 'looked after' by a local authority. Consequently, the code of treatment, described in Chapter 6, will apply (except for the rules relating to parental contributions). As far as family contact is concerned, the department is in the same position as the designated police officer, so that a fairly wide discretion is given.

The SSD has more than just a duty to accommodate, however, because the invocation by the police of their protection power triggers off an obligation on the part of the department to mount an investigation into the child's case. This is laid down by section 47. According to this, the enquiries are to be directed in particular towards establishing whether it would be in the child's best interests for an emergency protection order to be sought.

The position of the parents

The position of the child's parents during the period of police protection, which, it will be recalled, can last for up to 72 hours, is inevitably rather weak. Although they have a statutory right to be informed of the situation, they lose whatever possession rights they had: a criminal offence is committed if they knowingly take the child away 'without lawful authority or reasonable excuse' (section 49). In practice, this will mean obtaining permission from either the police or the social services department. And although the Act refers to contact with the child, it is ultimately a matter of discretion for the authorities. Furthermore, there is no right of appeal against the exercise of their powers by the police. The only consolation is that the period of protection will have a relatively short life. If it is superseded by the making of an emergency protection order, the parents will be in a position to challenge that order (and it should be noted that in these circumstances the eight day maximum duration of an emergency protection order runs from the first day of police protection).

Police applications for emergency protection orders

Since emergency protection orders can be made on the application of any person, it follows that they may be sought by the police. This subject is discussed in Chapter 8.

The role of the police in assisting officials

The Children Act contains a number of provisions, modelled on existing legislation, under which the assistance of the police can be sought. The theme running through these provisions is the need to facilitate police involvement when the exercise of statutory powers by public officials, notably social workers, is being frustrated, or is likely to be frustrated. Knowing when police assistance will be helpful, and knowing when it will be counter-productive, are obviously matters for professional judgement, and not surprisingly the Act maintains a neutral stance: it makes assistance possible but does not compel its deployment.

The Act (the relevant sections are 48 and 102) uses common criteria for the situations in which it authorises the issue of a warrant of assistance: *either* it must appear to the court that a person attempting to exercise powers has been prevented from doing so by being refused entry to the premises concerned or refused access to the child concerned *or* it must appear to the court that any such person is likely to be so prevented from exercising powers. The situations in question concern the exercise of the following powers:

1 Powers under an emergency protection order.
2 Powers under Part VII (inspection by local authorities of

accommodation provided by voluntary organisations).
3 Powers under Part VIII (inspection of registered children's homes).
4 Powers under Part IX (inspection of private foster homes).
5 Powers under Part X (inspection of premises used for child minding or day care).
6 Powers under section 80 (inspection of children's homes etc. by representatives of the Secretary of State).
7 Powers under section 86 (inspection by local authorities of residential care homes, nursing homes and mental nursing homes).
8 Powers under section 87 (inspection of independent schools).
9 Powers under Schedule 3 (visits by and contact with a supervisor under a supervision order).
10 Powers under section 33 of the Adoption Act 1976 (visiting of protected children).

In each of these cases, the court may direct that the constable concerned may be accompanied by a doctor, nurse or health visitor if he so chooses. The person applying for the warrant is entitled to accompany the constable, unless the court has directed otherwise. What the warrant does is to authorise (not compel) the constable to assist the applicant in the exercise of the powers concerned. This may obviously involve the application of a certain amount of force. Once the assistance has been given, and entry to the property or access to the child secured, the situation may demand the exercise of other police powers, e.g. the power of arrest.

Police involvement in the recovery of abducted or missing children

Section 50 of the Children Act permits the court to make a 'recovery order' in respect of various types of child: those who are the subject of a care order or emergency protection order and those who are in police protection. The order can be made whenever there is reason to believe that the child has been unlawfully taken away, or is being unlawfully kept away, or has run away, or is staying away, from the person who for the time being has care of him under the relevant arrangements. The order can also be made if there is reason to believe that the child is missing. The effect of a recovery order is to authorise the police, among others, to remove the child. They may also enter any premises specified and search for the child. In addition, any person who has information as to the child's whereabouts is required to disclose that information to the police if asked to do so.

Section 50 is a useful provision but its scope is obviously limited. It should be borne in mind, however, that it forms only one part of child abduction law. There is plenty of other legislation on the subject (e.g. the Child Abduction Act 1984).

10 Care orders

Introduction

Part IV of the Children Act is entitled 'Care and Supervision' and, as the title implies, it contains provisions concerning care orders and supervision orders. Because the effects of these two orders are so different, it is proposed to deal with them separately in this book. The present chapter is devoted to care orders.

In Part IV of the Act, the crunch question is reached, so far as State intervention in family life is concerned: in what circumstances are parents and other care-givers liable to have their children forcibly removed from their care, perhaps for good? The grounds for a care order are supremely important in the context of the Children Act, because the statute goes out of its way to channel all local authority applications for compulsory care through this procedure. No longer will separate grounds exist where care is being sought during matrimonial or other family proceedings. Nor will the wardship jurisdiction be available, as it is at present, as a convenient method of by-passing the statutory procedure. All cases in which long-term intervention is being considered will need to be studied with reference to Part IV.

In addition to the grounds for an order, other important questions arise. Who may apply for an order? What will the procedure be? What is the effect of a care order? What rights of appeal exist? All of these matters, and many others, have been up for review and debate during the past few years; the consequences may be seen in Part IV.

Applicants for a care order

Only a local authority or an authorised person can apply for a care order (section 31). 'Authorised person' will in practice continue to mean the NSPCC, now expressly mentioned in the legislation, and if it proposes to make an application, it is required to consult the local authority in whose area the child is ordinarily resident. The Act, however, prevents the NSPCC applying if the child is already the subject of an application for a care or supervision order; nor can it apply if the child is subject to a supervision order. In these situations, a local authority will by definition already be involved and accordingly intervention by the NSPCC would be inappropriate.

The rules just described mean that local education authorities and the police will lose their existing powers to apply for care orders. There are a number of reasons for this change. One reason is that a care order will vest parental responsibility in the social services authority; that being so, it is only right that it should make the decision whether or not to seek an order. In addition, the removal from the legislation of the specific care order conditions relating to education and the commission of an offence (see below) renders LEA or police initiation open to question. The Child Care Law Review saw some advantage in 'ensuring from the outset of what may become a long history of compulsory intervention that the social services department are in the lead and firmly identified by themselves and others as having the primary responsibility for the child'. The power of the NSPCC to institute care order proceedings is admittedly inconsistent with such arguments, but its special position is justified by the role it has come to play in child protection matters. Even so, the Act recognises the central position of the social services department by requiring the NSPCC to consult it before taking action, and by specifying certain situations in which the Society cannot act at all.

The children concerned

Any child under the age of 17 can be the subject of a care order application, with the exception of a sixteen year old who is married (section 31).

The grounds for a care order

According to section 31(2), a court may only make a care order if it is satisfied:

> (a) that the child concerned is suffering, or is likely to suffer, significant harm; *and* (b) that the harm, or likelihood of harm, is attributable to (i) the care given to the child, or likely to be given to him if the order were not made, not being what it would be reasonable to expect a parent to give to him; or (ii) the child's being beyond parental control.

Four very important definitions accompany section 31(2). 'Harm' means ill-treatment or the impairment of health or development; 'development' means physical, intellectual, emotional, social or behavioural development; 'health' means physical or mental health; and 'ill-treatment' includes sexual abuse and forms of ill-treatment which are not physical. In addition, section 31(10) states that 'where the question of whether harm suffered by a child is significant turns on the child's health or development, his health or development shall be compared with that which could reasonably be expected of a similar child'.

These grounds are, of course, very different from the existing grounds set out in section 1 of the Children and Young Persons Act 1969. They are also different from the grounds for a parental rights resolution set out in section 3 of the Child Care Act 1980. And they are different from the grounds for a committal to care order set out in various matrimonial and family proceedings legislation.

A great deal of thought has gone into the wording of the new grounds. They are based largely on the recommendations of the Child Care Law Review, which expressed the view that 'the primary justification for the State to initiate proceedings seeking compulsory powers is actual or likely harm to the child'. It rejected proposals to have a simple test based on the welfare of the child on the grounds that this would lead to widely varying and subjective interpretations and would fail to offer the right degree of statutory protection against unwarranted intervention. The welfare of the child is important, and, as we shall see, it forms part of the decision-making process, but on its own it is not enough to justify intervention. Conditions of greater specificity are needed: hence section 31(2).

Very careful consideration will have to be given to section 31(2) in cases where compulsory intervention is being mooted. Inevitably, it contains a number of interpretation issues. 'Harm' is defined expansively, particularly through its incorporation of impairment of development; but, to give the court jurisdiction to make an order, it must be shown that the harm is 'significant'. *There is no definition in the Children Act of 'significant'.* This word has been included in the statutory formula to emphasise the gravity of compulsory intervention and to warn the court that an order should not be made in trivial cases. Of course, it may be said that no harm suffered by a child is trivial, especially harm caused by physical violence or sexual abuse (which is specifically mentioned in the definitions). It may also be said that no court would ever make a care order unless the case was a serious one. No doubt there is a lot of truth in this. The fact remains, however, that with the very broad meaning attributed to 'harm' in the Act, some sort of qualifying term is warranted to prevent unnecessary interference. At any rate, this was how the Government argued it. The Lord Chancellor put it this way:

> It is not proper to intervene on any level of harm. The fundamental point is that State intervention in families in the shape of the local authority should not be justified unless there is some level – 'significant' is a good word for it – at which significant harm is suffered or is likely to be suffered

Whether or not the harm is 'significant' is ultimately for the court to decide, guided no doubt by relevant expert evidence. It will be noted that where the allegation is that harm is impairment of health or development – as opposed to ill-treatment – the section requires the child's health or development to be compared with that which could reasonably be expected of a similar child, i.e. a child of the same age, characteristics, disabilities, etc. The degree of disparity between the child before the court and the hypothetical similar child will determine whether the harm is significant or not.

The section talks not only of significant harm which is being suffered, but also of significant harm which is likely to be suffered. This is important. One of the most serious shortcomings of the Children and Young Persons Act 1969 is its concentration on the present. One result has been that local authorities have felt obliged to resort to wardship proceedings to protect a child who has not yet been harmed but who can reasonably be expected to be if nothing is done. Cases where harm is anticipated are now covered by the care order grounds. So a child who is presently in a safe environment, a hospital, for example, or a foster home or a children's home, can be made the subject of a care order application where it can be shown that if he goes home to his family, significant harm will probably ensue.

Proof of harm, or the likelihood of it, is not enough to authorise the making of a care order, however. The second limb of section 31(2), paragraph (b), has to be satisfied as well. So the applicant must show either that the harm is attributable to the child's being beyond parental control – this partly reflects the existing law – or that the harm is attributable to the standard of care given or likely to be given to the child if the order is not made. If this last condition is relied upon, it must be shown that the standard is different from that which it would be reasonable to expect a parent to give him. In this situation, the applicant and the court will have to focus on the particular attributes of the child and measure them against the standard of parenting that can be offered by the care-giver (or prospective care-giver in an anticipated harm case). Different attributes will obviously require different standards, and the applicant will have to prove a substantial shortfall in those standards to get its order.

This second limb is clearly necessary, for if it, or something like it, were not in the Act, it would technically be possible for a court to make a care order in completely inappropriate circumstances, for example where harm is being suffered but that harm is in no way due to any inadequacy on the part of the carer, e.g. where it is caused by the unavoidable actions of a third party. And it should be observed that where the requirements of the limb are satisfied, that in itself does not suggest any culpability on the part of the carer: it may simply be a case of him not having the necessary faculties to care for or control the child.

The new grounds and the old grounds compared

The new emphasis on 'harm' will inevitably mean that some of the situations which currently qualify for compulsory treatment will no longer do so. Taking the Children and Young Persons Act 1969 first, cases where the child's proper development is being avoidably prevented or neglected would tend to fall within the new grounds; but cases involving 'moral danger', the child being beyond parental control, absence of education or the commission of a criminal offence may well not, certainly they will not do so automatically. These latter conditions were criticised by the Child Care Law Review as leading to confusion, arbitrariness and injustice; it was said that, far from operating to protect families against unwarranted intervention, they 'may have the opposite effect and operate as magnets for drawing children within the sphere of compulsory care'. Similar arguments were deployed in relation to some of the grounds for assumption of parental rights resolutions under the Child Care Act 1980, for example the ones concerning parental incapacity and the habits or mode of life of the parent. It was suggested that 'the section 3 grounds, by focusing on parental unfitness, may have a stigmatising effect which may itself provoke unnecessary conflict and be detrimental to all concerned by unnecessarily prolonging proceedings and adding to their traumatic effects'. As for the existing committal to care grounds in family proceedings, these were condemned as unacceptably vague, being based on 'exceptional circumstances'.

In future, therefore, no 'harm' will mean no care order. It should be noted, however, that the unavailability of a care order will not necessarily preclude some other type of legal procedure being invoked. For example, absence of education which is not productive of significant harm will be able to be dealt with under the new education supervision order provisions (on which see Chapter 12). And for children in long-term accommodation who need substitute parents (who might currently be dealt with by the section 3 resolution procedure), the procedures relating to guardianship (see Chapter 2), adoption and residence orders under section 8 (see Chapters 3 and 4) may supply the solution.

In abolishing the device whereby parental rights may be assumed in respect of a child who has been in voluntary care for three years, the Children Act effects a sharp reversal of the policy contained in the Children Act 1975. This is a deliberate move. The Child Care Law Review condemned the three year ground as: 'arbitrary in individual cases, looking neither to the child's needs nor to how they can be met. The need of a child in this category for an effective parent can in our view best be met through proceedings in private law.' The general thrust of this argument is no doubt correct. But substitute legal parents may not always be available, and if this is so and if the natural parents are off the scene, there may well be practical problems for an authority looking after a child. Without a care order, it will lack parental responsibility and as a result it may be inhibited in taking certain types of action vis-a-vis the child for fear of acting illegally. Recourse to legal advice will be necessary where the social services department is unsure of its powers (for further discussion, see page 75).

When an application can be made

Section 31(4) states that an application for a care order may be made on its own or in any other family proceedings. By this, the Act simply means that an application can be made whether or not any other legal proceedings involving the family are on foot. If other 'family proceedings' are in train, the local authority or the NSPCC can apply in them. The Act defines these 'other proceedings' as meaning:

1   Proceedings under Parts I and II of the Act (e.g. a guardian's application or an application for a section 8 order).
2   Proceedings under the Matrimonial Causes Act 1973 (divorce, nullity and judicial separation).
3   Proceedings under the Domestic Violence and Matrimonial Proceedings Act 1976 (injunctions).
4   Adoption proceedings.
5   Proceedings under the Domestic Proceedings and Magistrates' Courts Act 1978 (maintenance applications).
6   Proceedings under the Matrimonial Homes Act 1983 (applications concerning the occupation of the matrimonial home).
7   Proceedings under Part III of the Matrimonial and Family Proceedings Act 1984 (applications for financial provision following an overseas divorce).
8   Wardship proceedings.

Whether or not any of these proceedings are in train at the time of the decision to go for a care order is, of course, purely a matter of chance, but if they are, it will often make sense for the care order request to be handled by the same tribunal.

The discretion to apply for a care order

It was emphasised in Chapter 7 that the decision to invoke the compulsory intervention machinery is essentially a matter for the discretion of the agency concerned, guided no doubt by a multi-disciplinary case conference. It follows that neither the local authority nor the NSPCC can be compelled to institute care order proceedings. Nor can they be prevented from doing so (except that, as previously mentioned, there are certain restrictions on the NSPCC). There is a provision in the Act, however, which enables an instruction to be given to a local authority to *consider* the launching of proceedings. This is section 37, which is concerned with family proceedings, understood in the sense described above (i.e. divorce, etc.), in which it appears to the court that it may be appropriate for a care order or supervision order to be made. In these circumstances, the court can direct the local authority to undertake an investigation of the child's situation.

Where such a direction is given, the local authority is under a duty to consider whether it should (a) apply for a care order or a supervision order, (b) provide services or assistance for the child or his family, or (c) take any other action. The local authority is perfectly entitled to decide not to take legal action, but if that is its decision, the Act requires it to inform the court of its reasons. The court must also be given details of any service or assistance which the local authority has provided, or will provide, for the family, together with details of any other action taken or to be taken. All this must be done within eight weeks of the direction, unless the court otherwise directs. Finally, section 37 requires an authority which declines to seek an order to consider whether it would be appropriate to review the case at a later date and, if so, to fix a date for the review. Whether or not the local authority decides to apply for an order, it may find that the care of the child is temporarily thrust upon it anyway, because section 38 of the Act enables a court which orders an investigation to make an interim care order at the same time. This matter is discussed later in this chapter.

The policy of giving discretion to agencies means the disappearance of the existing procedure prescribed by section 3 of the Children and Young Persons Act 1963, under which a parent can apply to the court for an order instructing the local authority to bring care proceedings on the 'beyond control' ground. The view which has prevailed is that, since it is the local authority which will gain parental responsibility for the child under a care order, it is only right that it should take the decision to set the machinery in motion. If a local authority declines to intervene, and this decision is regarded as mistaken, the parents (and others, for that matter) may be in a position to utilise the section 26 complaints procedure. This will depend, however, on the child concerned being 'in need' within the meaning of the Act (on which see Chapter 5).

The court's discretion to make a care order

The establishment of the harm grounds laid down by section 31(2) is an essential pre-requisite to the making of a care order. But that in itself is not, or should not be, at any rate, enough to obtain the order. The Children Act maintains the position under the existing law whereby once grounds are shown the court has a discretion whether or not to sanction intervention.

The exercise of this discretion is obviously a critical matter and the Act contains provisions whose object is to guide the court. These provisions are not, however, set out in Part IV, but at the beginning of the Act in Part I. The reason for this arrangement is that the guidelines are also applicable to the so-called private law procedures which were discussed in Chapters 3 and 4. One can see the sense in collecting general rules of this sort in the introductory part of the statute; the danger, though, is that they will be missed by the reader. Overlooking them could lead to very unfortunate results.

The first, and most important, guiding provision is section 1(1), which requires the court to regard the child's welfare as the paramount consideration. This represents no change in the existing law.

The second provision is section 1(3), which supplements the welfare principle by setting out a checklist of relevant factors to which the court should have regard. This checklist, which is not intended to be exhaustive, was discussed in Chapter 3.

The third provision is section 1(5). This states that the court is not to make the order 'unless it considers that doing so would be better for the child than making no order at all'. This particular rule was suggested by the Law Commission in the context of its study of private child law (see the discussion in Chapter 3). The Government decided, however, that it could usefully be employed in the public law field as well, so as to implement the recommendation of the Child Care Law Review that the legislation should require the court to be satisfied that the order contemplated is the most effective means available to it of safeguarding and promoting the child's welfare. What this rule seeks to do in the present context, therefore, is to ensure that a compulsory order is only made by the court where it is convinced that that order, as opposed to any other way of disposing of the case, will bring positive benefits. The onus of showing these benefits will, of course, lie on the local authority (or the NSPCC if it is bringing the case).

The processing of a care order application

The procedural aspects of legal proceedings can be dry and technical, and therefore off-putting to non-lawyers. Technical they might be, but they are also important. Their potential for determining the course which a case takes is significant and often underrated. In the context of care order proceedings, a sound knowledge of the basics is essential for child care social workers, in order to develop effective working relationships with the child, his family and the various professionals involved in the case (including the agency's own lawyers). Many individuals caught up in care proceedings need constant reassurance and explanation of the various stages which the case will go through. Social services staff are ideally placed to supply this.

Like the existing legislation, the Children Act does not attempt to lay down a comprehensive procedural code for compulsory intervention proceedings. Most of the procedural rules will be made outside Parliament by specially appointed committees of lawyers. The official description given to these rules is 'Rules of Court' and each type of court is governed by its own set of rules. At the moment, care orders under the Children and Young Persons Act 1969 can only be made by the juvenile court; hence the fact that the procedural rules are entitled the Magistrates' Courts (Children and Young Persons) Rules. Under the Children Act, it will be possible for care order applications to be dealt with either by the magistrates' court, or by the county court, or by the Family Division of the High Court (this 'concurrent jurisdiction' is discussed in Chapter 13). Consequently, one may expect three sets of Rules of Court to be formulated. Notwithstanding the reliance on rules, the 1989 Act is not completely silent on procedure. On certain matters, it contains specific provisions, whilst on others it contains indicators of what is expected in the rules.

Participation in care order proceedings

Tremendous, and unnecessary, problems have occurred in this area under the existing legislation. The root cause of the problem is the quasi-criminal reference in the Children and Young Persons Act 1969 to the local authority 'bringing a child before' the juvenile court, with the result that in law the principal parties are the local authority and the child. This is a nonsense, of course, since in practice if anybody is being 'brought before' the court, it is the parents. It is, after all, their 'rights' which will be affected by an order. This distortion of reality has had severe effects on the ability of parents to participate fully in care proceedings and appeal against any order made. It is true that the Children and Young Persons (Amendment) Act 1986 introduced some improvements in relation to their participation; it also made provision for grandparents – another neglected category – to become parties to proceedings. That Act, however, was always recognised as a purely interim response to the problem, to be swept away in due course by comprehensive legislation.

In the event, the Children Act is a damp squib on this issue. Section 93 simply states that 'rules of court may make provision as to the persons entitled to participate in proceedings under this Act'. So everything will be done by secondary legislation. As with all the other sets of rules and regulations, the precise content had not been worked out when the Act was before Parliament. All that we have to go on are the snippets offered by Government spokesmen during the debates. According to these, the child will be a party in every case and persons having parental responsibility for the child will 'normally' be parties. As regards others, it is unlikely that the rules will restrict the existing categories, and so grandparents may be expected to receive a specific mention as well. Beyond this it is difficult to go, but it is to be hoped that the rules are suitably generous.

It should be noted that under section 93, the rules can draw a distinction between participation as a party, which will carry with it the ability to call evidence, cross-examine witnesses and appoint an advocate, and participation which merely involves making representations to the court.

The appointment of a guardian ad litem for the child

This matter is dealt with in Chapter 14. In summary, though, it may be noted that section 41 of the Children Act requires the court to appoint a GAL for the child in every care order case unless it is satisfied that it is not necessary to do so in order to safeguard his interests. This is yet another area, however, where supplementary rule-making by government will have a substantial impact.

Timetables

Reference has already been made to the provisions in the Act which concern delays in private law proceedings (see Chapter 3). There are equivalent provisions for public law proceedings. Section 1(2) applies, so that a court hearing an application for a care order must have regard to the general principle that any delay in disposing of the application is likely to prejudice the welfare of the child. In addition, the court is required by section 32 to draw up a timetable 'with a view to disposing of the application without delay' and to give 'such directions as it considers appropriate for the purpose of ensuring, so far as is reasonably practicable, that that timetable is adhered to'. The Rules of Court may specify, inter alia, timescales in relation to certain stages in the proceedings.

Nobody could reasonably object to these provisions, which may do something to eradicate the appalling delays which often occur in care proceedings. A key factor, though, is resources, both within the local authorities (social services and legal departments) and the court system, and that particular matter is completely beyond the scope of the Act. As a result, one may be forgiven for viewing them with the tiniest degree of scepticism.

During the passage of the Act, the Government announced that the processing of legal aid applications in respect of care proceedings would be altered with a view to curbing delays.

The local authority's plans for the child

During the passage of the Children Act, the Government announced that it intended the Rules of Court to require a local authority to provide the court with details of its proposals for the child should the care order be granted. Such a requirement is seen as meshing in with the duty of the court, already noted, to ensure that making an order would be better than not making one. To decide this matter, the court will obviously need to know what the local authority expects to do with the child and a plan will convey this information. The point has also been made that the presentation of a plan may be conducive to an agreement being reached with the parents about the need for an order. How much hard detail can go into this plan will clearly be dependent upon the circumstances, for example the degree of previous local authority involvement (and therefore knowledge of the family). It may be, and this was acknowledged by the Government, that the local authority's proposals may be in the nature of an embryo plan rather than a comprehensive one.

One specific aspect of the local authority's plans is regulated by the Act itself: parental contact. Section 34 contains an elaborate series of provisions on this difficult subject and these are considered below. At this stage, however, it is worth noting section 34(11). This states that before making a care order, the court must (a) consider the arrangements which the social services department has made, or proposes to make, with regard to contact and (b) invite the parties to comment on those arrangements. The singling out of this issue is a clear reflection of the importance which has been increasingly attached to it.

Before we leave this subject, the point should perhaps be made that, while plans and proposals will have to be produced to the court, there is no question of the local authority being forever tied to them. As we shall see, it is a cardinal principle of the new public law framework that case management is principally a matter for the social services department rather than the court. Once the child is in care the department's overriding duty will be to promote his welfare; if that demands a deviation from the arrangements previously indicated to the court, then the department should not feel inhibited about following this course. The Committee of Inquiry into the Tyra Henry case (*Whose Child?* (1987)) recommended that the means by which a department proposed to implement a care order should be annexed to the order and that if any 'significant change' was proposed the court's consent should be obtained. This was an interesting recommendation but it ran directly counter to the Department of Health's views on the allocation of functions in children's cases, so it is not surprising that it has been rejected.

The legal effect of a care order

The legal consequences of compulsory care under the existing statutory framework are not easy to describe in straightforward terms. There are two main reasons for this. The first is the existence of three, completely separate, compulsory procedures (care orders under the Children and Young Persons Act 1969, committal to care orders under the family proceedings legislation and assumption of parental rights resolutions under the Child Care Act 1980) whose respective effects are stated in different terms. The second lies in the very obscurity of the effects as stated. As we have seen, the aim of the Children Act is to construct a single compulsory care procedure. This effectively eliminates the first cause of the present confusion. As for the second, it may be thought that the Act achieves as much certainty as can reasonably be expected from a piece of legislation.

Parental responsibility

The principal effects of a care order are described in section 33 of the Children Act. Under section 33(1) it is the duty of the local authority to receive the child into its care and to keep him there while the order remains in force. Under section 33(3) the local authority 'shall have parental responsibility for the child'. This brings us back to the introductory part of the Act, where the concept of parental responsibility is defined as: 'all the rights, duties, powers, responsibilities and authority which by law a parent of a child has in relation to the child and his property' (section 3). In principle, therefore, the social services department acquires through a care order the complete range of parental 'rights' recognised by English law (on which see Chapter 2). First and foremost amongst these, and a driving force behind many care order applications, is the right to decide where the child is to live. Not every parental right, however, is transferred, because section 33 excepts certain specific matters from the general rule:

1 The local authority shall not cause the child to be brought up in any religious persuasion other than that in which he would have been brought up if the order had not been made. This repeats the existing law. There was some misunderstanding of this provision during the passage of the Act and it should be emphasised that the section does not prevent a change of religion if the child wishes this to occur. All it does is to prevent the SSD taking the initiative and imposing an alteration on the child.

2 The local authority does not acquire rights in relation to adoption. Here, too, the existing law is preserved. While the natural parents retain the right to veto an adoption, this is subject to the power of the adoption court to dispense with their consent.

3 The local authority does not acquire the right to appoint a guardian for the child. If a guardian is appointed by the natural parents (on which see Chapter 2) and he assumes parental responsibility on their death, the local authority's position is not prejudiced in any way, because the care order will remain in force during these events. The guardian's 'rights' will be subject to those of the authority. As will be seen, however, the guardian will fall within the contact provisions of the Act and he cannot therefore be ignored. He will, moreover, be in a position to apply for the discharge of the care order.

4 The local authority does not acquire the right to effect a change of surname. The Act states that while a care order is in force nobody may change the child's surname without either the written consent of every person who has parental responsibility or the leave of the court. Whilst the local authority gains parental responsibility under a care order, the parents retain it, and so if they (or either of them) object to a change in the name of the child, the local authority must obtain permission from the court.

5 Although parental responsibility will give the local authority the right to decide where the child is to reside, if it (or anybody else) wishes to remove him from the UK, the same requirements apply as for a change of name, i.e. written consent or the leave of the court (the UK, incidentally, means England,

Wales, Scotland and Northern Ireland, it does not include the Channel Islands and the Isle of Man). The only exception is where the authority plans to remove the child for less than a month: this will facilitate holidays abroad with schools and foster parents, etc. There are special arrangements for the permanent emigration of care order children and these are dealt with below (see 'the code of treatment').

Subject to the above-mentioned exceptions, then, the general effect of a care order is to deprive the parents of decision-making power in relation to the upbringing of their child. They do not lose their 'parental responsibility', this only happens on adoption, but their ability to exercise it as they think fit is caught by the provision in section 2 which states that the fact that a person has parental responsibility shall not entitle him to act in any way which would be incompatible with any order made with respect to the child under the Act. Just to put beyond doubt the ascendancy of the local authority, the Government put into the Act a provision (section 33(3)) which states that the authority shall have the power to determine the extent to which a parent or guardian of the child may meet his parental responsibility for him. It is only to exercise this power where it is satisfied that it is necessary to do so in order to safeguard or promote the child's welfare.

Of course, when a care order is made, the court is not always starting with a blank sheet of paper. What is the position when orders have already been made in respect of the child? The orders most relevant here are the section 8 orders described in Chapters 3 and 4, especially those concerning residence and contact. There may, for example, be a complex network of such orders in force made in a succession of matrimonial hearings. The Children Act (section 91) imposes a simple result: the making of a care order discharges any section 8 order automatically. Past orders can therefore be ignored.

The new contact provisions

The law relating to access to children in compulsory care affords a classic illustration of the complicated and confused way in which our public child care regime has developed over the years. For a long time, there was no legislation directly on this matter at all, which meant that, certainly for care order children and section 3 resolution children, the social services department had virtually a free hand in the matter of regulating access. Some parents who were denied access attempted to deal with the problem by making their children wards of court, in the hope of persuading the High Court to impose an access requirement on the department. However, in a series of controversial cases the judges declined to allow the wardship jurisdiction to be used by parents (or others, e.g. relatives) in this way.

Eventually, specific legislation was enacted: the Health and Social Services and Social Security Adjudications Act 1983 (HASSASSA). The 1983 Act enables applications to be made to the juvenile court for access orders in relation to children in compulsory care and it directs the Department of Health to issue a Code of Practice. But this 'reforming' legislation was quickly exposed as unsatisfactory in a number of respects. For example, it is only concerned with cases in which access is completely terminated or refused: it is useless in cases (and there are many of them) where it is the *amount* of access which is being questioned. Relatives are excluded from the scope of the Act. In addition, the drafting is in many respects less than satisfactory, which has caused problems of interpretation.

HASSASSA and the Code of Practice are swept away by the Children Act and they are replaced by a completely fresh set of provisions, modelled on the carefully considered proposals of the Child Care Law Review. There is reason to believe that this time, Parliament has got it right. The approach of the Act could be said to be two-pronged. On the one hand, there are provisions of a general variety, applicable to all children who are being looked after by a local authority, which are designed to encourage family contacts. On the other hand, there are the very specific provisions geared to care order children.

The general provisions

Some of these have already been mentioned in Chapter 6 in relation to children who are accommodated under section 20 (i.e. under voluntary arrangements). It will be recalled that Schedule 2 of the Act requires the local authority to endeavour to promote contact between the child and his parents, any non-parent having parental responsibility, any relative or friend, and 'any other person connected with him', unless it is not reasonably practicable or consistent with his welfare. The location of the child's residence is obviously a vital factor in the contact context, and section 23(7) of the Act, repeating the existing law, requires that the accommodation provided shall be 'near his home', subject to the usual considerations of practicability and welfare. Schedule 2 pushes this theme a stage further by requiring the local authority to take reasonable steps to keep the child's parents (and any non-parent with parental responsibility) informed of his present address. Again, though, this is qualified: if the authority has reasonable cause to believe that informing them would prejudice the child's welfare, the duty does not apply. Finally, there is provision made in Schedule 2 for the payment by the local authority of travel expenses etc. incurred by parents and others in visiting the child (and vice-versa).

All these provisions are important and helpful, particularly the first one, but they only go so far. Without more, the position of parents, relatives and other interested parties in the matter of contact would be wholly dependent upon the view of the case taken by the social services department. There are no doubt social services professionals who would be inclined to support a drawing of the line at that point, but the pro-access movement has had its effect over the years and there was never really any question of Parliament going back on the HASSASSA approach of giving parents 'rights' in this area. The Cleveland episode simply served to reinforce this. Consequently, we must now turn to the specific, rights-oriented, contact provisions in the Children Act.

The specific provisions

Section 34 contains the specific provisions (the contact order provisions in Part II of the Act, described in Chapters 3 and 4, are not available for care order children). It aims to encapsulate and extend the present provisions, including those of the Code of Practice, and it does this by imposing a duty on the local authority to allow reasonable contact, by giving interested parties the opportunity to test the authority's plans and decisions in court, and by giving the court ample powers both at the time of the making of the care order and subsequently.

Looking at this matter from a temporal angle, the question of future access should first arise for discussion during the care order proceedings themselves. Section 34(11) is quite explicit on this point:

> Before making a care order with respect to any child the court shall – (a) consider the arrangements which the authority have made, or propose to make, for affording any person contact with a child to whom this section applies; and (b) invite the parties to the proceedings to comment on those arrangements.

So the local authority will be expected to arrive at the court hearing with proposals relating to contact: the matter will have to be directly addressed in the run-up to the case. How detailed the proposals can be must, of course, be dependent upon the particular facts, but the department should be prepared for rigorous questioning from all sides on the extent to which it plans to provide contact arrangements for the child. In deciding whether or not to make the order, the court will obviously take these proposals into account.

The Act goes further than this, however, by enabling the court to attach to a care order specific access conditions. This is a significant departure from the existing law, which only permits court control of access *after* an order has been made and *after* access has been refused or terminated by the department. The Child Care Law Review recommended this particular reform. 'We understand', they said, 'that the delay between a denial of access and its coming to court is often a matter of months and given the crucial effects of interrupted access we have concluded that any disagreement about it should be identified and dealt with as early as possible in the history of each case.' Section 34 enables the court to make 'such order as it considers appropriate with respect to the contact which is to be allowed' with the child. Conditions can be imposed if the court thinks they are warranted, so that for example the start of contact could be delayed for a period, or the court could stipulate that a certain individual must, or must not, be present during contact periods. Maximum flexibility is achieved through this simple device.

However, there are restrictions on the circumstances in which a contact order can be made. The court is given the power to make an order of its own motion, i.e. without anybody formally applying for one. Such an order can be in favour of any named person. Short of this, though, a contact order needs to be applied for. If the social services department or the child makes an application, the court may order contact in favour of any named person, whether related to the child or not. What of applications from other parties? On this, the Act draws a distinction between those who are entitled to apply and those who can only apply with the leave of the court. Those entitled to apply are the child's parents (this includes the unmarried father), any guardian, any non-parent who holds a residence order in respect of the child and any non-parent who has been given care and control in wardship proceedings. Relatives, therefore, are required to obtain the leave of the court before applying for contact, unless they hold a residence order or have care and control through wardship. This requirement is not uncontroversial, but the Government held to the view that it was necessary to prevent unwarranted interference. It should not, in fact, be that difficult for relatives to get leave. Other parties might find the requirement more of a barrier, depending on their relationship with the child.

In addition to making an order for contact, the court can make one against it. It has the power to make an order authorising the department to refuse to allow contact between the child and his parent(s), guardian or any non-parent who holds a residence order or has care and control through wardship. This power is necessary because, as will be seen shortly, there is a general obligation on the part of the local authority to allow these persons reasonable contact once a care order has been made. It can be exercised on an application made by the department or the child himself; alternatively, the court may make a refusal order of its own motion. Again, conditions can be attached by the court as appropriate, so that for example a limited time-scale could be built in, or the court could give the local authority the power to deny contact in certain specified circumstances.

What is the position regarding contact, then, when a care order has been made? The answer to this depends on whether or not the court has attached any specific provision to the care order. If it has not done this, section 34(1) applies. This states that, following the making of a care order, the local authority shall allow the child 'reasonable contact' with his parents (including the unmarried father), any guardian, anybody who held a residence order immediately prior to the care order (the word is 'held' rather than 'holds' because the effect of a care order is to discharge a residence order) and anybody who had care and control through wardship. So we have here a statutory presumption in favour of reasonable contact, confined, though, to the categories mentioned. The Act recognises, however, that contact may sometimes have to be curtailed, and it therefore permits (section 34(6)) the local authority to refuse contact if it is satisfied that it is necessary to do so in order to safeguard or promote the child's welfare and the refusal is decided upon as a matter of urgency and does not last for more than seven days. This time restriction puts the onus on the SSD to apply to the court for an order authorising continued refusal of contact with the person or persons concerned. Such an order may also be sought by the child.

If the parents (or guardian etc.) feel that the local authority is not providing 'reasonable' contact, they can apply to the court for a specific order; so can the child himself. Indeed, others can do this – relatives, for example – although they first have to get the leave of the court to intervene. An alternative – and opinions may differ as to how attractive an option this is – is for the aggrieved person to utilise the complaints procedure which the local authority will have to establish under section 26.

If specific contact arrangements have been ordered by the court as part of the care order package, then the position is that the duty to provide reasonable contact to those in the specified categories remains, but it is subject to the arrangements made by the court. So if, for example, the court when making the care order authorised the local authority to refuse contact with the child's father, the authority would still have the duty to allow the child reasonable contact with his mother, subject, though, to its power to refuse contact for up to seven days, and its power to go to court and ask for an order authorising continued refusal. If the court has made an order for contact, the same power to suspend the arrangements for up to seven days is given to the local authority. This power, not dissimilar to the one under the existing law, will be useful in those cases where the court has been persuaded to make a contact order but the working of it in practice proves disastrous so that urgent action is called for.

Several other features of section 34 deserve a mention. Firstly, all orders of the court regarding contact can be varied or discharged subsequently. Secondly, where an application to court has been refused (including an application for variation or discharge), another application cannot be made by the unsuccessful party within six months without the leave of the court. Thirdly, while the existing Code of Practice will disappear, Government regulations will be made in relation to contact. These are likely to regulate in particular the way in which local authorities use the seven day suspensory power and the extent to which the local authority and the parties concerned may by agreement deviate from any order made by the court.

To summarise the contents of this very important section, then, the intention is to enable contact arrangements to be worked out at the time of the care order, to give parents and others with parental responsibility a presumption in favour of contact coupled with the right to apply to the court if dissatisfied, and to give the local authority a sufficient degree of control to act in the best interests of the child with the same sort of access to the court as the parents have got. Section 34 represents a very substantial advance for the interests of parents (including unmarried fathers) and, therefore, as some would say, the interests of children in care. It is indeed a far cry from the pre-1983 position. Moreover, in so far as it gives non-parents the right to apply to the court, it also represents a notable advance for the wider family, whose claims could be said to have been rather neglected by the legal system over the years. Quite clearly, its provisions, taken with the other, more general, provisions of the Act, will require even more attention to be directed by social services departments and by judges and magistrates to the contact issue than before.

It is the expressed view of the Government that recourse to the courts to resolve questions of contact should only occur in exceptional circumstances. It is pinning its hopes on SSDs using their general duty under Schedule 2 to promote contact in such a way as to provide satisfaction for all concerned.

The treatment of the child in care

In Chapter 6, we saw how children who are provided with accommodation by a local authority under section 20 arrangements become subject to the code of treatment contained in sections 20–29 and Schedule 2 of the Children Act. This code is also applicable to children 'in care', i.e. those who are the subject of a care order. As was mentioned in Chapter 6, this arrangement is no different in principle from the existing law, because the Child Care Act 1980 deals simultaneously with those received into care under that Act and those committed to care under compulsory powers.

It is not proposed to rehearse all the contents of this code in the present chapter, the reader is referred to Chapter 6 for a description and commentary. It is very important to note, however, that the two groups of children, accommodated children and care order children, are not treated by the Act in exactly the same way in every single respect. Differences exist in certain key areas. Such differences as there are have come about for a variety of reasons, but one of them is fairly obvious: in a care order case, it will necessarily have been shown to the satisfaction of a court that the child was suffering, or was likely to suffer, significant harm attributable either to a shortfall in parenting standards or to the child's being beyond parental control. With that as a backcloth, special safeguarding provisions are clearly necessary. The features of the code of treatment which bear especially on care order children are as follows:

• The local authority's duty to keep the parents notified of the child's residence is qualified. This provision, described earlier (see page 120), is obviously required for those cases where a persistent parent, for whatever reason, needs to be kept well away from the child.

• Parents have no entitlement to remove the child from secure accommodation (as do the parents of accommodated children). This is simply a consequence of the central thrust of the care order, which is to vest the right to decide the child's residence in the local authority. Having said this, secure accommodation remains subject to stringent criteria (see page 57).

• There are special rules concerning emigration (Schedule 2). The local authority can arrange this, but the arrangement can only go ahead with the approval of the court. The Government can give approval under existing legislation but the view now is that the court should be involved on account of the gravity of the matter. Schedule 2 lists a number of conditions on which the court must be satisfied, one of these being the consent of those with parental responsibility. This consent, however, can be dispensed with by the court on three grounds (taken from adoption law): the person cannot be found, is incapable of consenting or is withholding consent unreasonably.

• The regulations which will be made under section 26 concerning reviews are likely to include a requirement under which the local authority is to consider whether an application should be made to discharge the care order. They are also likely to include a requirement under which the child is to be told of the steps he may take under the Act. One of the 'steps' an older child might take, or at least consider, is applying to the court himself under section 39 for a discharge of the order.

● While the local authority has a range of options available in the matter of accommodation, there are special provisions (in section 23(5)) concerning the release of the child back into the care of his parents: the authority may only allow him to live with a parent (or a non-parent with parental responsibility or the former holder of a residence order) in accordance with regulations made by the DoH. This rule is based on the existing law. The word 'existing' is just about appropriate here, because the first set of regulations made by the Government, the Accommodation of Children (Charge and Control) Regulations 1988, only came into force in June 1989. This whole area of legal control is a recent development, having originated in the Children and Young Persons (Amendment) Act 1986. That Act was a private member's measure, partly inspired by the Jasmine Beckford tragedy, and it brought 'home on trial' arrangements within central government control for the first time (the original intention was for the local authority to obtain court agreement to the return of the child, but amid widespread opposition from child care organisations the DoH insisted on a modification). The 1989 Act endorses such an approach. The working of the Charge and Control Regulations is likely to be closely monitored by the Government in the period leading up to the implementation of the Act, in order to see whether any amendments are required. It would be unwise to assume that the 1988 regulations will simply be repeated, particularly in view of their novelty.

Case management: who is in charge?

In the light of the preceding discussion, now may be an appropriate stage to take an overall look at the position of the social services department in relation to the care order child and consider the extent to which it, rather than the court, is in control of his case management. This is a fundamental issue which has been keenly debated in recent years (e.g. during the enactment of the 1986 reforms on charge and control, referred to above).

There are various reasons for this but one of them is undoubtedly the growth in the use of wardship by local authorities. Wardship has been invoked in many cases as a result of the unsatisfactory features of care proceedings under the Children and Young Persons Act 1969, a state of affairs which the Children Act attempts to rectify, of course. A by-product of this, whether intended by the local authorities or not, has been that they have, in respect of the children concerned, become subject to the general wardship rule that no important step can be taken in relation to the ward without the court's consent. Furthermore, the wardship court has explicit statutory powers to issue directions to the local authority as to the exercise of its responsibilities to him. This continued court involvement in child care cases, which not infrequently means a succession of journeys back to court for permission to do this or that, has not always proved popular with social services departments, but it has nevertheless attracted considerable support, with the result that there has been pressure from some quarters to extend the principle into care proceedings generally.

Both the House of Commons Social Services Committee and the Child Care Law Review came out against the idea of general judicial supervision of care order children. According to the latter:

> the court should be able to determine major issues such as the transfer of parental rights and duties where there is or may be a dispute between parents and local authorities, while the management of the case should be the responsibility of the local authority ... it is necessary that the body with day to day responsibility for the child should have a positive duty to 'take a grip on' the case and make firm and early decisions without the temptation to pass responsibility to another body.

The House of Commons Committee took an even stronger line. It felt that SSDs cannot be viewed simply as agents of the court. A mandatory requirement of regular court supervision would, in its view, paralyse local authorities and lead to a reduction of staff morale, quite apart from dividing the care of children between yet more adults in different organisations.

In the event, and perhaps inevitably, the Children Act reveals some ambivalence on this question. Once a care order is made, decision-making is handed over to the social services department. In relation to all types of decision, the department is obliged to ascertain the wishes and feelings of the child and his parents (and others, see page 61), so far as is reasonably practicable, and give due consideration to them. In relation to some types of decision, however, the department is subject to direct court control. These have been mentioned in the preceding pages of this chapter, but to summarise, they are:

1 decisions on contact;
2 decisions on secure accommodation;
3 decisions on change of name;
4 decisions on removal of the child from the UK for longer than one month;
5 decisions on emigration.

It is not being suggested here that the intervention of the courts in these matters is unjustified. Each of the decisions in the list is important. What may be difficult to sustain, however – certainly as a matter of logic – is the drawing of the line at these particular points.

If a local authority needs the consent of the court before arranging a six week trip overseas for the child, why is no consent needed before moving him to long-term foster parents at the other end of the county? If the court can impose conditions regarding contact, or secure accommodation, why should it not be able to regulate medical treatment? There is no completely satisfactory answer to such questions. The effect of the Children Act, like the existing legislation, is to leave both the court and the local authority with hands on the steering wheel, although at certain stages in the journey one of them must relinquish control to the other. In some cases, e.g. those involving decisions on contact, the authority may not welcome the prospect of court interference. Conversely in others, e.g. where it wishes to see rehabilitation being pursued vigorously, the court may regret not having the ability to issue directions, as opposed to exhortations. Opinions will obviously differ as to whether the balance of power created by the Act is an acceptable one.

Before leaving the issue of case management, we should note that, whether or not the court has powers of direct control on any particular matter, every decision of the social services department is subject to potential scrutiny through the section 26 complaints procedure and also through the local ombudsman system. In addition, the special judicial review jurisdiction of the High Court, which covers all public bodies, is available for cases in which the department can be said to have failed to perform a statutory duty, or exercised its discretion in a perverse fashion, or followed a procedure which is grossly unfair to those affected by the decision. While a strong case needs to be made out on judicial review, there have been several well-publicised instances of successful challenges to child care decisions in recent years (e.g. the case in 1986 in which the court ordered a social services department to reconsider its decision to abandon tentative rehabilitation plans for a care order child on the grounds that the parent concerned had not been given the opportunity to refute unsubstantiated allegations made against him by a third party, allegations which resulted in the department's decision). The signs are that this particular form of redress will be increasingly used in the future.

What, however, will not be available when a care order is made are the procedures in Part II of the Act relating to contact orders, prohibited steps orders and specific issue orders (described in Chapters 3 and 4). The ability of the court to make such orders against a local authority would be inconsistent with the more specific, care order-oriented, framework described in this chapter. Residence orders, on the other hand, are a different matter; they are considered in the following section.

The duration of a care order

Unless it is brought to an end earlier, a care order will continue in force until the child reaches the age of 18 (section 91). This represents a change in the existing law. The Children and Young Persons Act 1969 provides for a care order to continue until the age of 19 if the child is over 16 at the date of the order; it also permits the juvenile court to order an extension to 19 where the child is in residential accommodation and there are reasons arising out of the child's mental condition or behaviour which warrant this. These rather anomalous provisions, which are not mirrored in the other existing compulsory procedures, are now swept away.

There are a number of methods by which the care order can be brought to an end prior to the statutory expiry date. These are as follows:

1 The court discharges the order following an application by the authority, the child or any person having parental responsibility.
2 A residence order is made by the court under section 8 of the Act.
3 The child is adopted.
4 The child is freed for adoption.

The first two methods call for comment. With regard to **applications for discharge**, the persons having parental responsibility (apart from the authority itself, of course) will normally be the parents of the child, or the mother if the parents are unmarried and no steps have been taken to vest responsibility in the father. The Act (section 39) gives the court power to substitute a supervision order for the care order, as an alternative to simply discharging the care order. The court also has the power to make a section 8 order (e.g. a contact order in favour of a foster parent, or a residence order in favour of an unmarried father or a grandparent). This is a good example of the way in which the Act usefully merges the private law orders with the public law ones, a matter discussed in the next section.

Under section 91, once an application is made, whether for simple discharge or for the substitution of a supervision order, no further application may be made for another six months without the leave of the court. As the Child Care Law Review observed: 'a balance has to be struck between fairness to applicants, the freedom of social workers to manage the case with foresight and the interests of the child in not being unnecessarily disturbed'. Needless to say, applications for discharge of a care order will be governed by the welfare principle in section 1 of the Act and the checklist of factors will also apply. Participation in the proceedings will, as in the original care proceedings themselves, be regulated by 'rules of court'.

Sustained efforts were made during the passage of the Children Act to incorporate a provision giving the court power to order the discharge of a care order while postponing its implementation. The object was to enable the court to direct a phased rehabilitation of the child with a view to reducing the adverse effects on the child of a sudden removal from care. Under the existing law, the High Court can achieve this sort of result thanks to its flexible wardship jurisdiction. The Government resisted this proposal, even though it had received support from the Child Care Law Review, on the grounds that it would interfere excessively with the case management functions of the social services department. Its view was that where phased rehabilitation was desirable, it could be achieved by the department through the exercise of its powers in relation to the child (e.g. generous contact coupled with home-on-trial arrangements). When everything was in place ready for the child's permanent residence at home, an application for discharge could, and should, be made. Opinions will differ as to whether the Act draws the line between court control and local authority control at the right place in this matter. It is worth remembering, however, that parents looking for a discharge order in the future may be in a position to work towards that goal with the court's help, by making use of the strengthened contact provisions in the Act. In other words, while the court is unable to direct a phased rehabilitation, it is able to order increasing contact vis-a-vis the child, the effect of which may be to enhance the prospects of an ultimate application for discharge of the care order being successful. This can be done whether the SSD agrees or not.

Finally, it should be noted that the facility of applying for a discharge order is going to make a specific appearance in the Government's review regulations (see page 125).

With regard to **residence orders**, these may be sought either by parents or by non-parents (see Chapters 3 and 4). In the latter category, foster parents and relatives obviously spring to mind as potential applicants where the child is in care. At present, these persons can apply for custodianship. However, as we saw in Chapter 4, the Children Act imposes various restrictions on non-parental applications; in particular, the leave of the court or the consent of the SSD may have to be obtained first, depending on the circumstances of the case. Parents, on the other hand, are entitled to apply for residence orders, and in view of the effect of such orders, there is no real difference from their point of view between applying for the discharge of the care order and seeking a residence order in respect of the child. There is one important exception to this, however. Whilst the unmarried father without parental responsibility may not apply for discharge of a care order, he does have the right to apply for a residence order, which, if granted, will supersede the care order. In this way, unmarried fathers have finally been given the chance to win the control of their children who have been taken into care.

The effect of all these provisions will be to increase considerably the flexibility of the court's powers when a care order has outlived its value. The introduction of the four types of section 8 order into the discharge process is particularly noteworthy in this respect; it should mean that the court is much better equipped than it is under the existing law to deal with the infinitely varying situations which arise in practice and should reduce the number of occasions on which it is necessary to launch a multiplicity of proceedings in order to achieve the desired end result.

The making of other orders on a care order application

When the court is invited to make a care order by a local authority or the NSPCC, it has a discretion in the matter even though the statutory harm grounds are proven. The range of orders which are available to the court, however, extends beyond simply the one being sought. The Children Act, repeating the existing law, enables the court to make a supervision order instead of a care order (section 31(5)); but it also enables the court to make one or more of the section 8 orders. This latter power (derived from section 10) is new, and it has been made possible by the manner in which the Act integrates the public and private law frameworks, something which is sadly lacking in the existing legislation.

What this means is that in future the court will be in a position to refuse, or adjourn, an application for a care order but at the same time make, say, a residence order in favour of a grandparent or aunt and uncle who have intervened in the proceedings on hearing about them (the new participation rules should allow for this). Alternatively, it could refuse a care order but combine a supervision order with a section 8 order. Under existing law, separate legal proceedings would have to be started to achieve results like these, an absurd waste of time and money. If the care order application is a many-sided contest, it makes sense for the one court to be given all the tools it needs to reach a result which is both practicable and in the child's best interests. The Act makes a welcome breakthrough in this respect.

The discretion of the court is not entirely unfettered, however, when it comes to the question of making section 8 orders in care order proceedings. Under section 38(3), where the court makes a residence order in such proceedings, it must also make an interim supervision order unless it is satisfied that the child's welfare will be satisfactorily safeguarded without one. The assumption being made here is that even if the child is not going into care, some sort of social work support and supervision will be called for, in view of the fact that the local authority or the NSPCC must have felt, when starting the proceedings, that compulsory intervention was necessary. The interim supervision order will enable social workers to keep an eye on the child's circumstances and perhaps return to the court for further measures if the residence arrangements do not work out.

Interim care orders

Section 38 of the Children Act empowers the court to make an interim care order in two situations. The first is where an application has been made for a care order or a supervision order and that application is adjourned by the court. The second situation is where there are family proceedings (e.g. divorce) before a court and the court decides under section 37 to order the local authority to investigate the possibility of applying for compulsory powers.

The court has complete discretion whether or not to grant an interim order, but it can only do so if it satisfied 'that there are reasonable grounds for believing that the circumstances with respect to the child are as mentioned in section 31(2)'. In other words, the court has got to be satisfied that there is reason to believe that the harm grounds needed for a full care order are present. It may turn out in the end that the harm grounds are not actually satisfied, but if at the interim stage there are reasonable grounds to believe this, the court has power to make the order. In exercising its discretion, the court should be guided by the same principles, set out in section 1, as apply to the making of a full order, i.e. the welfare principle (including the checklist of relevant factors) and the principle that an order should only be made if it will produce positive benefits for the child.

Interim orders, by definition, are only short-term measures: they are not designed to be an end in themselves but simply a stop-gap. At the same time, however, they can have a critical effect on the family concerned. To prevent their abuse, time limits are necessary, and the Children Act constructs these by using the device of listing a number of events and stating that an interim order will cease to have effect where any of these events first occurs. The starting point is that an interim order will last for as long as the court says but it cannot in any circumstances last for more than *eight weeks*. This upper limit was regarded by the Child Care Law Review as more realistic than the existing 28 day maximum. If the application for a full order is disposed of within that time, the interim order will lapse at that earlier time. If the interim order is a second or subsequent such order, it can only last for *four weeks*, unless it was made less than four weeks after the first order, in which case it can last until eight weeks from the first order.

The normal pattern, therefore, where successive interim care orders are made, is for an initial eight week limit to apply, followed by limits of four weeks. It can be seen that the eight week initial period links in with the time which is normally to be given to a local authority under a section 37 investigation order. Where the court reduces the investigation time-scale, however, the maximum duration of any interim order it makes will be reduced too. So if the court in family proceedings orders a local authority investigation to be completed within, say, a fortnight, an interim order made could only last for that time (further interim orders could, however, be made if the local authority, having carried out its enquiries, decided to apply for compulsory powers).

While the Children Act preserves the present power to make successive orders, the accepted view is that these are not to be encouraged. The Child Care Law Review noted research findings indicating that such orders are common – indeed, one case was reported to have involved a total of fourteen interim measures – but emphasised the dangers of delay, particularly the unsettling effect it can have on the child. Moreover, as time ticks away, the parents' position is inevitably placed in greater jeopardy. As was well said by a High Court judge recently, 'in children's cases delay can stultify – indeed, almost completely nullify – the benefit of a right to be heard'. It is to be hoped, therefore, that agencies and courts will take on board the clear message contained in the Act about delays in children's cases. It will be recalled that section 32 sets out specific timetabling provisions on the matter. These do apply to interim orders. Nor should it be forgotten that government rules will be made under that section with a view to curbing delays. The interaction of such rules with the time limit provisions of section 38 will need to be borne in mind very carefully by all practitioners. Having said this, it remains the case that lengthy delays and numerous adjournments in child care cases are sometimes unavoidable; for example, this is yet another area where the resources issue looms large. The Children Act encourages, but does not guarantee, a solution to these problems.

The legal effect of an interim care order

The legal consequences of an interim care order are identical to those of a full care order, except for the limited duration factor. The reason for this is that section 31 of the Children Act defines 'care order' so as to include an interim order, so that the provisions in the Act which spell out the effects of a 'care order' automatically extend to interim measures (unless there is any express provision to the contrary). There is nothing novel about this rule, the Children and Young Persons Act 1969 says much the same thing, but of course the Children Act does contain new provisions about the consequences of care orders, notably parental contact. Because of section 31, these apply equally to interim orders.

The important and crucial effect of an interim care order will therefore be to vest parental responsibility in the local authority, with the result that it will be in a position to exercise parental powers in relation to the child (subject to the specified exceptions). In exercising these powers, it will be subject to the code of treatment for children in care but it will not be subject to court directions, except with regard to three matters. The first is parental contact. The contact provisions in section 34, described earlier, are fully applicable to interim orders and thus increase the protection of parents' and other parties' interests (the denial of access under interim care orders was, of course, a major issue in the Cleveland affair).

The second matter is the medical and psychiatric examination of the child. According to section 38, on making an interim care order, or subsequently, the court may give such directions as it considers appropriate with regard to such examinations or other assessment; and the direction may be to the effect that there is to be no examination or no examination unless the court directs otherwise. A direction can be varied at any time. The rationale for this power is presumably twofold: in some cases, its exercise will facilitate the effective disposal of the case (for example, the local authority may be reluctant to use its parental responsibility to force an examination on the child); secondly, an examination is considered such an intrusion from the civil liberties point of view that the local authority should not have a completely free hand at the interim stage (even if it will have if a full order is made). This is another spin-off from Cleveland, as is the important supplementary rule that if the child is of sufficient understanding to make an informed decision he may refuse to submit to an assessment. This is identical to the rule applicable to emergency protection orders, discussed in Chapter 8.

The final matter on which there will be court control is secure accommodation. As with the contact provisions, those in section 25 concerning secure accommodation are equally applicable to interim orders.

Discharge of interim care orders

The rules here are the same as for full care orders, so that an application for discharge can be made either by the local authority, the child, or any person having parental responsibility. If an application fails, the six month rule relating to full orders (see page 129) does not apply, so further applications may be made freely.

After-care

The after-care provisions of the Act (contained in section 24) apply to care order children in the same way as they apply to accommodated children. They are described in Chapter 6.

11 Supervision orders

Introduction

The term 'supervision order' has many connotations under the existing law and it will continue to have many under the Children Act. The Children and Young Persons Act 1969 provides for the making of supervision orders both in criminal proceedings against a young offender and in care proceedings in respect of children at risk. Matrimonial and other 'family' legislation also provides for the making of supervision orders, but the legal effects of these differ from the effects of orders made under the 1969 Act. Even within the 1969 Act there are differences, since supervision orders made in criminal proceedings can contain special conditions which are not available in care proceedings.

The effect of the Children Act is to replace the rules relating to supervision orders made in care proceedings and family proceedings. Criminal supervision orders remain governed by the Children and Young Persons Act 1969, a result which furthers the aim of the new legislation to hive off the law relating to young offenders into a completely separate and self-contained code.

In Chapters 3 and 4 it was seen how the 1989 Act enables a family assistance order to be made in family proceedings. This type of order can only be made with the consent of the parties concerned and its main object is to facilitate the provision of fairly short-term social work support to the family following marital breakdown. A supervision order, on the other hand, is a form of compulsory intervention – albeit less drastic in its effects than a care order – which is designed for cases with a child protection element where a wider range of supervisor's powers may be needed. Nor should the supervision order be confused with the 'education supervision order' created by the Act. That order, described in Chapter 12, is designed for truancy cases only and is governed by a separate set of rules. To summarise, the following forms of supervision will be available through a court order after the 1989 Act:

1 A supervision order made under the 1989 Act.
2 A supervision order made in criminal proceedings under the 1969 Act.
3 An education supervision order.
4 A family assistance order.

The present chapter is devoted to the first type of order: a supervision order made by the court on grounds of harm, or likely harm, to the child. The provisions of the 1989 Act touching criminal supervision orders are discussed in Chapter 18.

During the passage of the Children Act, there was comparatively little discussion or debate on the question of supervision orders in care proceedings. The general impression conveyed was that the subject is uncontroversial. If this is indeed the case, one of the reasons is no doubt the limited amount of intervention which the making of such an order involves: a supervision order, unlike a care order, does not give the social services department parental responsibility for the child. A further reason may be the limited use of such orders in practice. The House of Commons Social Services Committee reported in 1984 that 'there are very few supervision orders made on welfare grounds' (as opposed to criminal grounds), although it did consider that an extension of their use to protect children would be beneficial, given that 'many children legally in care are in practice at home and in all but name under supervision'.

The provisions of the Children Act concerning supervision orders reflect the recommendations of the Child Care Law Review, which drew attention to a number of defects in the existing law, particularly the absence of any power to impose requirements directly on the child's carer (as opposed to the child himself).

Matters on which the rules coincide with those for care orders

In a number of respects, the Act treats supervision orders and care orders in an identical fashion. These are listed below. Each of the matters in the list is discussed in the previous chapter.

- Applicants for an order.
- The children concerned.
- The grounds for an order.
- When an application can be made.

- The discretion to apply for an order.
- The court's discretion to make an order (although it should be noted that the Act reveals a strong bias towards the making of a supervision order when a residence order is made in care proceedings).
- The processing of an application.
- The making of other orders on a supervision order application. This means that a care order could be made instead of a supervision order; a section 8 order could also be made, either instead of or alongside a supervision order (but the Act does not allow a residence order or a contact order to be made in favour of a local authority).

The legal effect of a supervision order

According to section 31(1), a supervision order is an order putting the child under the supervision of a designated local authority or of a probation officer. The legal framework of this 'supervision' is set out partly in section 35 and partly in Schedule 3 at the back of the Act. This arrangement, perhaps familiar to readers by now, is simply the draftsman's way of making the provisions more digestible: the idea is that the more basic rules are put in the section, with the detail relegated to the Schedule.

The basic duty of the supervisor

Section 35 states that while a supervision order is in force it shall be the duty of the supervisor to advise, assist and befriend the supervised child. This represents no change in the existing law. In carrying out this duty, the social worker has almost unlimited discretion in the sense that the terms used – 'advise' etc. – are not defined or regulated in any way (although note the possibility of government regulations being made on this, a matter discussed later in this chapter).

Other duties of the supervisor

Section 35 imposes two other duties on the supervisor. The first is to take such steps as are reasonably necessary to give effect to the order. The second duty arises where the order is not completely complied with or may no longer, in the supervisor's opinion, be necessary. In these circumstances, the supervisor is required to consider whether or not to apply to the court for a variation or discharge of the order.

Selection of the supervisor

There is no change on this point. The supervisor will be the local authority, unless the authority requests the appointment of a probation officer and an officer is already working (or has worked) with another member of the child's household.

Requirements which may be included in an order

Schedule 3 of the Children Act follows the existing law by specifying various types of requirement which the court may insert into a supervision order. These requirements, however, are more extensive than those currently available. The possibilities are as follows:

- The child is to live at a place or places as directed by the supervisor for a specified period or periods.
- The child is to present himself to a person as directed by the supervisor at specified places on specified days.
- The child is to participate in activities as directed by the supervisor on specified days.
- The 'responsible person' – this is any person having parental responsibility for the child or any other person with whom the child is living (e.g. relatives or private foster parents) – is to take all reasonable steps to ensure that the child complies with any direction given by the supervisor. The responsible person has to consent to this requirement: the Government's view is that the effectiveness of supervision orders will depend upon co-operation between the supervisor and the family ('there would be little purpose in imposing a requirement that a person should seek to ensure that a child complies with directions unless that person consented').
- The responsible person is to comply with any directions given by the supervisor requiring him to attend, with or without the child, at a specified place for the purpose of taking part in specified activities (the responsible person has to consent to this requirement). The Child Care Law Review mentioned child care classes and mother and toddler groups as examples of 'specified activities'.
- The responsible person is to take all reasonable steps to ensure that the child complies with any requirement relating to medical examinations or treatment (again, consent is needed).
- The responsible person is to keep the supervisor informed of his address if it differs from the child's.
- The child is to keep the supervisor informed of any change in his address.
- The child is to allow the supervisor to visit him at his place of residence.

The hallmark of these requirements is flexibility: none of them has to be included in a supervision order and many of them lend themselves to being specially adapted to fit the features of the case. Some will be applicable to children of all ages, others will only be useful where the child is reasonably mature. Where the supervisor is authorised to issue directions, there is discretion both in the issuing of the directions and in defining their precise content. This is the social worker's discretion, not the court's. The only limitation is that the total number of days in respect of which the child or the responsible person can be required to comply with directions cannot exceed 90 or such lesser number as the court fixes. As the Child Care Law Review observed: 'although intermediate treatment has usually been provided with offenders in mind, it may be equally applicable to children in need of care.'

Duties of the responsible person

Whatever the requirements built into the order, the Act enables the supervisor to demand details of the child's address from the responsible person (assuming it is known) and requires that person to allow the supervisor reasonable contact with the child. These are important new provisions.

Psychiatric and medical examinations and treatment

Given that supervision orders will be made only in cases involving actual or anticipated harm, the question of health examinations and health treatment assumes considerable importance. Schedule 3 of the Act contains special rules on these matters.

As far as **examinations** are concerned, the Act enables the court to incorporate in the order a requirement that the child is to submit to a medical or psychiatric examination or a requirement that the child is to submit to any such examination 'from time to time as directed by the supervisor'. Any examination is to be conducted – and the order must specify this – either by a named medical practitioner, or at a named establishment at which the child is to attend as a non-resident patient, or at a health service hospital (or, in the case of a psychiatric examination, a hospital or mental nursing home) at which the child is to attend as a resident patient. This last option is only available in cases where the court is satisfied on expert evidence that the child may be suffering from a physical or mental condition that requires, and may be susceptible to, treatment, and that a period as a resident patient is necessary if the examination is to be carried out properly.

Two general restrictions are imposed on the making of medical examination requirements. First, the court must be satisfied that satisfactory arrangements have been, or can be, made for the examination. Second, where the child has sufficient understanding to make an informed decision, the court must be satisfied that he consents to the inclusion of the requirement. This is an interesting concession to the self-determination ideas discussed in the Gillick case in 1985.

Turning to **treatment**, the Act draws a distinction between psychiatric and medical cases. In both cases, the court is enabled to include in the supervision order a requirement that the child shall submit to such treatment as is specified for such period as is specified (note that it is the court which orders the treatment, not the supervising social worker). The treatment must be given by a named practitioner, or else received by the child as a non-resident patient at a specified place, or as a resident patient in a health service hospital (or, in psychiatric cases, in a hospital or mental nursing home). The common condition which must be met for a treatment requirement is that the court is satisfied on expert evidence that the condition of the child is such as requires, and may be susceptible to, treatment. In psychiatric cases, the court must also be satisfied that the child's mental condition is not such as to warrant his detention in pursuance of a hospital order under the Mental Health Act 1983.

The same general restrictions as apply to examination requirements apply to treatment: satisfactory arrangements for the treatment must be in hand and a child who has sufficient understanding must consent to the inclusion of the requirement.

Once treatment gets under way, circumstances may change. New facts may come to light, for example. The Act caters for this by providing for a written report to be sent by the medical practitioner in charge of the child's treatment to the supervisor if he becomes unwilling to continue to treat the child, or if he forms the opinion that the treatment should be continued beyond the specified period, or that the child needs different treatment, or that the child is not susceptible to treatment, or that the child does not require further treatment. If such a report is sent, the supervisor must refer it to the court, which may then cancel or vary the requirement (e.g. by extending the period of treatment) depending on the circumstances.

Duration of supervision orders

According to Schedule 3 of the Act, a supervision order will last for one year in the first instance. This represents a change in the law, as under the Children and Young Persons Act 1969 a supervision order can be made for up to three years. The Government's view is that the shorter duration will 'make orders more effective, induce a greater sense of purpose and reduce the risk of undermining parents' confidence in relation to their children'. The supervisor can, however, apply to the court for one or more extensions up to a three year period.

If the child reaches the age of 18 before the statutory expiry date, the order automatically lapses. Similarly, a supervision order can be discharged in advance of the expiry date by the court on the application of the supervisor, the child, or any person having parental responsibility. To deter groundless applications for discharge, section 91 of the Act provides that at least six months must elapse between such applications unless the leave of the court is obtained. If a care order is made in respect of a supervised child, the supervision order is automatically discharged.

Variation of the supervision order

Care orders cannot be varied but supervision orders can be. This can be done so as to alter the requirements which have been included in the order, e.g. by inserting a requirement authorising directions to be given by the supervisor, or inserting a requirement concerning medical examinations or treatment. Such variation can be sought by the same persons who can apply for discharge (see above). In addition, a variation can be sought by a person with whom the child is living, even if that person could not apply for discharge. This would enable somebody such as a relative who is caring for the child to apply for a variation of any requirement which had been imposed on him as a 'responsible person'.

Interim supervision orders

The interim supervision order is a novelty, since it does not feature in the existing legislation. Section 38 is the governing provision and the rules it prescribes are essentially the same as the ones pertaining to interim care orders (on which see Chapter 10). One difference is worth noting, however: although the court generally has a discretion whether or not to make an order, section 38(3) states that where, on an application for a care order or supervision order, the court makes a residence order, it shall also make an interim supervision order, unless satisfied that the child's welfare will be satisfactorily safeguarded without an interim order being made. The reasoning behind this was described earlier (see page 131).

It is also worth noting that none of the special provisions relating to psychiatric and medical examinations and treatment in Schedule 3 applies to interim supervision orders. Instead, section 38 itself contains rules (described in Chapter 10).

DoH regulations concerning supervision

Schedule 3 repeats the existing law by enabling government regulations to be made 'with respect to the exercise by a local authority of their functions where a child has been placed under their supervision by a supervision order'. The power to make regulations in this area was created by the Children Act 1975 as a direct result of the majority recommendations of the Committee of Inquiry into the Maria Colwell case. That Committee drew attention to the fact that, whereas boarding out arrangements were governed by an elaborate set of rules, statutory supervision was subject to none (it is interesting to note that the new Charge and Control Regulations, introduced in June 1989, have arisen out of an identical argument). It felt that, in view of the serious shortcomings disclosed by the evidence in that case, some of the provisions in the Boarding Out Regulations could be usefully applied to social workers undertaking supervision work, at any rate in 'Maria-type cases' where a care order based on harm is later discharged and substituted with the lesser order.

In fact, such regulations have never been made, and it may be that the chances of them being made have been reduced by the provisions of Schedule 3 of the Children Act, which themselves introduce a generally tighter legal framework into this area.

Obstruction of the social worker

The legal effect of the new supervision order provisions will be to involve parents and other carers much more directly: not only can requirements now be imposed on them by the court (with their consent), the Act itself imposes obligations – to inform the supervisor, on demand, of the child's address and also to allow the supervisor reasonable contact with the child. Where the supervising social worker meets with obstruction, the legal sanctions which can ultimately be applied need to be fully understood. It is not being suggested that they should be resorted to as a matter of routine, but their availability, and the skilful communication of their availability to the child's carers, can play a significant part in converting obstruction into co-operation.

The Children Act makes no change in the existing law as regards sanctions for non-compliance with requirements, which means that disobedience can be punished by the imposition of a financial penalty, and, in the county court and the High Court, the imposition of penalties for contempt (supervision orders will, of course, be available from these two courts under the concurrent jurisdiction provisions of the Act). In addition, it will be open to the local authority, if there is severely obstructive behaviour, to return to the court with a request for a care order.

If action has to be taken in an emergency, then the fact that a supervision order has been made will not prevent the supervisor, the NSPCC, the police or others from utilising the various intervention procedures established by the Act. The use of these procedures will be necessary to effect a forcible removal of the child, since a supervision order does not give this power. In this connection, mention should be made of the provision in the Act which is specifically geared to the obstruction of a social worker acting under a supervision order. This is section 102 (also discussed in Chapter 9), which enables the court to issue a warrant authorising any constable to assist a person in the exercise of certain specified functions. One of these functions is the entitlement of a supervisor to have reasonable contact with the child, laid down by Schedule 3. So if entry to the child's residence, or access to the child within his residence, is denied, it will be possible for the supervisor, via a court order, to call upon the police for assistance. This enforcement mechanism is not really new since the Children and Young Persons Act 1969 was amended in 1983 along similar lines.

Supervision order or care order?

As we have seen, the Children Act injects a very large element of discretion into the procedures relating to care orders and supervision orders. This discretion operates at two levels. At the agency level, there is discretion as to whether to apply to the court at all, and if so, which order to seek; and at the level of the court, once the harm grounds are proved, there is discretion as to which order, if any, to make.

After the Act, there will continue to be cases in which the arguments for and against a particular type of order (or combination of orders) are finely balanced. No piece of legislation could reasonably be expected to provide the answer to such dilemmas and the Act does not seek to do so. As always, the 'right' course of action is a matter for professional judgement. The same goes for applications to the court to vary or discharge an order already made.

12 Education supervision orders

Section 36 of the Children Act creates a new type of order aimed solely at school attendance cases: the education supervision order. This innovation is a direct result of the recasting effected by the Act of the grounds for a care order, whereby school non-attendance no longer features (expressly, at any rate) in the situations which can give rise to compulsory care. The reasons for this alteration were discussed in Chapter 10. The removal of non-attendance from the grounds for a care order or supervision order required the creation of some other welfare-based mechanism for truancy cases. The Government's answer is the education supervision order (ESO).

ESOs will be sought by, and administered by, education departments. They will be available (at the discretion of the court) where the child concerned is of compulsory school age and is not being 'properly educated', which means not receiving efficient full-time education suitable to his age, ability and aptitude and any special educational needs he may have. This is very close to the existing formula employed in the care order provisions of the Children and Young Persons Act 1969. The social services department must be consulted before the making of the application. This requirement is important, for it acknowledges the fact that some – indeed, many – truancy cases involve wider problems which may be more appropriately handled by social services, rather than education, social workers. While education is no longer specifically mentioned in the care order provisions, it is quite possible for 'harm' to encompass impairment of development brought on by, inter alia, an absence of proper education. This would open up the prospect of using the compulsory care procedure in order to tackle the family's situation. The Review of Child Care Law, which recommended the new framework, stated that 'we would hope to see continuing co-operation between education departments and social services departments'.

The effect of an ESO

Schedule 3 of the Act supplements section 36 by spelling out the effect of an order. The supervisor is obliged to advise, assist and befriend the child and his parents ('parent' here has the extended meaning given by the Education Act 1944), and to give them directions in such a way as will, in his or her opinion, secure that the child is properly educated. Before giving directions, the supervisor must, so far as is reasonably practicable, ascertain the wishes and feelings of these parties, including their wishes as to the place at which the child should be educated (this may not be a school), and give due consideration to them.

The order may require the child to keep the supervisor informed of his address, and it may require the child to allow the supervisor to visit him. Similarly, the parents must inform the supervisor, on request, of the child's address (assuming they know it) and, if the child is living with them, they must allow the supervisor reasonable contact.

Duration

The order will last for one year initially, but extensions of up to three years each will be possible, on the application of the education department. While the order is in force, it has the effect of superseding legal provisions which would otherwise apply. So that the parents' duty to secure the child's education is replaced by the duty to comply with the supervisor's directions; any existing school attendance order lapses; and the provisions in the education legislation concerning attendance orders and parental wishes and preferences become inapplicable. The order can be brought to an end in a number of ways: by the expiration of the one year period or an extension period; by the child reaching the age of 16; by the making of a care order; or by virtue of a court order discharging it (available on the application of the relevant parties).

What if the supervisor's directions are ignored?

If directions are not complied with, the supervisor is required to consider what further steps to take. The Act expressly mentions two possible steps. Firstly, a parent who persistently fails to comply with a direction can be prosecuted in the criminal courts and fined. Defences to this charge are available, including the defence that the direction was an unreasonable one. Secondly, in the case of persistent failure by the child, the education department must notify social services, which in turn must investigate the case. Further action may follow this.

Will the ESO work?

These new statutory provisions on school attendance come at a time of considerable change and anxiety in the education world. The education welfare service, which will play a crucial role in ESO administration, will be heavily affected by the progressive implementation of the Education Reform Act 1988. In addition, there is debate concerning the training and professional qualification needs of EWOs and their relationship with social services departments, to say nothing of the continuing controversy surrounding the efficacy of formal legal intervention in truancy cases. This sort of backcloth makes it particularly difficult to gauge the likely effect of the ESO.

The Government itself has acknowledged this. The Minister of Health told the House of Commons:

> I hope that the provision will be seen as a more sensible and sensitive way of tackling the problem. Whether it will work in practice we do not know. Many people who advised us believe that it will. We shall see.

The Education Act 1944

The creation of the ESO has made it necessary to amend section 40 of the Education Act, which deals with the prosecution of parents. This the Children Act does, and the result is that before proceeding against a parent, the education department must consider whether it would be appropriate, instead of or as well as instituting the proceedings, to apply for an ESO. In addition, the criminal court can direct the department to make such an application, although the department is not obliged to follow this direction if it thinks an ESO is not needed.

13 Courts and appeals against court decisions

The preceding chapters have explained how the Children Act creates a substantial number of legal procedures under which applications can be made to 'the court' for a variety of orders. As we have seen, these procedures have come to be categorised as either 'public' or 'private'. The primary purpose of the present chapter is to describe those provisions of the Act which are concerned with the courts having jurisdiction (i.e. power) to deal with these applications.

The concurrent jurisdiction principle

As it happens, the provisions of the Act dealing with the courts are reasonably straightforward, for this is yet another subject where the really detailed rules have been left to be formulated by the Government. According to section 92, for the purposes of the Act 'the court' means the High Court, a county court or a magistrates' court. This definition will normally apply wherever the Act refers to a 'court' and on the face of it it means that all the procedures described in this book can be initiated in any of the three courts mentioned, the applicant having a choice in the matter.

This sort of arrangement is certainly not new: adoption and custody applications, for example, can be made to all three courts under the existing legislation. From the social worker's point of view, however, probably the most significant consequence of section 92 is that it opens up the possibility of local authorities applying for care orders and supervision orders in the county court and the High Court. It also makes it possible for disputes concerning contact with children in care to be taken to these courts. Under the existing Children and Young Persons Act 1969 and the Child Care Act 1980, only juvenile courts (i.e. magistrates' courts) have the power to make orders. One of the beneficial consequences of the new jurisdiction rules will be to render it more likely that all the issues in any particular case can be resolved in one court. The present concentration of local authority applications in the juvenile court is an obstacle to this.

The subordinate legislation

Section 92 tells only half the story, however. As indicated above, the Government's intention is to supplement this provision by detailed orders. These will have the effect of depriving the applicant of complete freedom of choice of court in certain situations. All of this is authorised by Schedule 11, which permits orders to be made requiring specified classes of proceedings to be initiated in specified courts. The orders may also specify the circumstances in which proceedings are to be transferred from one court to another.

In view of the number of legal procedures created by the Children Act, it will not be surprising if these orders turn out to be fairly lengthy. It is certain that they will be amended from time to time to deal with particular problems which practical experience of the new regime throws up. The formulation of the orders will be a contentious matter, too, since the allocation of cases between courts raises delicate questions regarding the relative expertise of the decision-makers and the efficiency of the various court administrators, not to mention the cost to the public purse.

Some clues to the Government's thinking on the content of its proposed orders were provided during the Parliamentary debates. It was stated that the power to make orders would be exercised initially in relation to local authority care cases:

> the intention is to require care applications to begin in magistrates' courts, from where some would be transferred to higher courts ... The power to transfer will be governed by criteria dealing with the complexity, weight or importance of the case. They will also refer to the need for speed in dealing with cases so that, for example, a magistrates' court which for some reason was unable to give an early hearing could transfer the case to a neighbouring magistrates' court or to a county court if that would speed up disposal.

The Government also announced that it was exploring what could be done to strengthen links between local courts and that it was considering what central co-ordinating machinery was necessary to promote a consistent judicial approach and to monitor administrative effectiveness. To this end, it announced the appointment of a judge and central and local advisory committees who would seek to ensure an efficient transition to the new scheme.

The Parliamentary utterances referred to above are not binding on the Government and in any case, much remains to be worked out. For these and other reasons, it would be foolish to try to anticipate too closely the nature of the orders which will be made. Suffice it to say that whatever their form, the orders are bound to have a considerable impact on the practical operation of the new children's procedures (as well as adoption, which is also covered by Schedule 11).

A Family Court?

The effect of section 92 is to retain the present system whereby children's cases are spread across the magistrates' courts, the county courts and the High Court. Quite apart from the difficult question of case allocation between these courts, the inclusion of section 92 was bound to stir up the still deeper issue of the need for a proper unified family court in this country. Attempts to amend the Bill so as to facilitate the creation of such a court were duly made but they were resisted by the Government on the grounds that this was the wrong piece of legislation for the job, since it was only concerned with children, not families in general. What the Government did suggest was that the new provision creating concurrent jurisdiction between the three courts could be seen as a preliminary step towards the development of a more radical court structure, should the adoption of such a structure ever be deemed appropriate. These arguments have some force, but they are unlikely to satisfy the demands of those who have been persuaded by the case so eloquently made by the Finer Committee as long ago as 1974. In the words of one MP: 'there should be one court system that people can understand'. Sadly, this still seems a distant prospect.

Appeals against court decisions

In the private area of child law, rights of appeal have in the past been available fairly extensively. This position is preserved by the 1989 Act. In public law cases, however, there have been major problems, caused mainly by defects in the Children and Young Persons Act 1969: local authorities, for example, presently lack a right of appeal on the facts against the refusal by a juvenile court of a care order. Such problems are resolved by the Children Act in two ways. The first way arises out of the concurrent jurisdiction provisions of the Act, noted above. Care cases which are taken to the county court or the High Court will automatically attract appeal procedures under existing legislation: an appeal can be made to the Court of Appeal. The second way is to provide expressly for wide rights of appeal against any decision made by magistrates, including a decision to refuse an order. This is done by section 94 of the Act and the appeal will go to the High Court.

Two matters deserve special mention. First, no appeal will be possible from the making or refusal of an emergency protection order or any direction given under one. This is slightly misleading, however, because as we saw in Chapter 8, applications for discharge of an EPO will be possible at the 72 hour point. Second, appeals against orders concerning the transfer of cases from one court to another will be regulated by government rules. One may therefore expect restrictions here.

Protecting the child pending an appeal

As explained above, local authorities will in future be able to appeal against a decision of a court refusing to sanction compulsory intervention. In some cases, the child concerned will already be subject to an interim order of some sort and therefore under the authority's wing. Section 40 of the Act allows the court to preserve this position pending an appeal by the authority. This power is exercisable where the court dismisses an application for a care order or a supervision order. The section also extends to cases where the court grants an application to discharge a care order or supervision order. It may order that its decision is not to have effect pending an appeal. When continuing the status quo, the court can attach conditions, so that in this respect it has a role in case management.

14 Welfare reports and guardians ad litem

The development of the law concerning welfare reports in children's cases and the related matter of the appointment of guardians ad litem for children reveal many of the problems which have beset child law generally in modern times. The legislation is complicated and has arrived in a piecemeal and unco-ordinated fashion. Underlying the haphazard advance of the law has been the perennial problem of resources and the resulting need to prioritise issues in relation to the allocation of hard-pressed social work and legal personnel. From the social worker's point of view, the differences between providing a welfare report and acting as a guardian ad litem may often be ones of form only, rather than substance. In both situations, the social worker temporarily becomes an officer of the court and the purpose of the appointment is the provision of an independent, objective and detailed analysis of the child's situation and prospects, judged by reference to the proposals being put before the court by the parties. Despite the similarity of function, however, it is necessary for present purposes to maintain a distinction between the two areas, because the applicable rules are different.

Welfare reports

The subject of welfare reports will be governed in future by section 7 of the Children Act. This is a very simple provision. It enables a court which is considering 'any question with respect to a child under this Act' to ask for a report on such matters relating to the welfare of the child as are required to be dealt with. The request, which must, of course, be complied with, can be made either to a probation officer or to a local authority and an authority can arrange for any report to be compiled either by one of its own social workers or else by a third party (e.g. the NSPCC).

The court's discretion

It can be seen that under this provision, the court has a discretion, not a duty, to order a welfare report. This is for the most part a repetition of the existing law, although in every custodianship application under the Children Act 1975 a report has to be produced by the social services department. This particular requirement, always anomalous, will disappear (as, of course, will the custodianship procedure itself).

When a report can be ordered

It can also be seen that the court is given the power to order a report in a wide range of situations: whenever it is considering a 'question with respect to a child under this Act'. In practice, it is likely to be used most frequently in 'private' applications concerning section 8 orders and applications by unmarried fathers for parental responsibility (see Chapters 2 to 4). This is because the various 'public' law proceedings – applications for care orders, supervision orders, emergency protection orders, etc. – are subject to the separate guardian ad litem provisions of the Act (discussed below).

The contents of the report

The existing custodianship provisions require the social worker's report to cover, inter alia, the matters listed in the Government's regulations. This arrangement has now been adopted for reports generally, for section 7 enables the Government to make regulations specifying matters which, unless the court orders otherwise, must be dealt with in any report. It is likely that the checklist in section 1 of the Act will be used as a reference point when these regulations are drawn up, although no legislation could ever hope to be completely comprehensive when it comes to tabulating the relevant factors in children's cases.

The delivery of the report

As far as the other detailed mechanics of the welfare report operation are concerned – such as the way the report is to be made available to the parties and the putting of questions to its author – these will for the most part be set out in Rules of Court, made by the Government. Section 7 contains only two provisions on the subject, apart from the ones mentioned in the previous paragraph, both drawn from the existing legislation. The first states that the report may be made in writing or orally, as the court requires. The second states that the court may take account of any statement contained in the report in so far as it is, in the court's opinion, relevant to the question which it is considering, whether or not it is consistent with the strict rules of evidence. According to the Law Commission, this emphasises the fact that 'these are reports for the court and not evidence presented by one or other of the parties to the case'. Nevertheless, some concern was expressed in Parliament about the use of hearsay in welfare reports, and it was suggested that special safeguards should be built in in fairness to the parties. It may be that the Rules of Court will contain provisions on the point, although the Government seemed to prefer leaving the question to the court's discretion.

The timing of the welfare report is obviously important and this matter too will no doubt be regulated by the Rules. Nor should it be forgotten that the Children Act makes provision for timetables in children's cases (see page 24): these will need to be very carefully borne in mind by social workers when compiling reports.

Guardians ad litem

Background

Although the drafting of the Children Act has met with general approbation, at least one distinguished Parliamentarian has viewed the retention of the expression 'guardian ad litem' as regrettable, in that it is technical and legalistic and liable to be misunderstood by those members of the public not versed in Latin. The use of Latin terms is indeed a pernicious feature of the English legal system but it is probably the case that this particular term has become so firmly entrenched as to be irremovable.

The existing GAL provisions of the Children Act 1975 (fully implemented only in 1984) represent a classic irrational fudge between the need to introduce second opinions in care and related proceedings and the need to go easy on scarce resources. Under these provisions, the appointment of a GAL is made possible but it is limited to cases in which there is or may be a conflict of interest, and even then it is left to the discretion of the court; although the exercise of discretion is weighted in the case of an unopposed application to discharge a care order or supervision order. GAL appointments are, in addition, linked in a fairly complicated fashion to the questions of separate legal representation and legal aid provision for the child's parents.

The changes made by the Children Act

Section 41 of the Children Act introduces a framework which is at once simpler and stronger than the existing one, the sort of framework which many (including those in government) wished to see on the statute book in the 1970s. The appointment of a GAL will be mandatory in 'specified proceedings' unless the court is satisfied that an appointment is not necessary in order to safeguard the child's interests. The expression 'specified proceedings' is defined so as to cover the following:

(a) applications for a care order or supervision order;
(b) family cases where the court has ordered the local authority to investigate the child's circumstances and has made, or is considering whether to make, an interim care order;
(c) applications for the discharge of a care order or the variation or discharge of a supervision order;
(d) cases where the court is considering whether to make a residence order in respect of a care order child;
(e) cases involving contact with a care order child;
(f) applications under Part V of the Act (EPOs and CAOs);
(g) appeals against decisions involving care orders or supervision orders and related decisions, and decisions involving CAOs;
(h) any other proceedings specified by Rules of Court.

An obvious consequence of these provisions is that there will be a considerable increase in the number of GAL appointments. Although section 41 retains an element of discretion as to appointment, the emphasis is firmly directed towards GAL involvement. The Government's view, as expressed during the Parliamentary debates, was that 'the courts are unlikely to find many cases in which it would not be appropriate to appoint a guardian' (it thought that 'a straightforward case involving an older child who has already instructed his own solicitor' might not require a GAL). It estimated that GALs would be appointed in upwards of 90 per cent of cases falling within the specified categories.

The Rules of Court: solicitors and panels

One striking feature of the Children Act, noted in many parts of this book, is its reliance on government-made rules and regulations to supply the detail to fill out general principles it lays down. The GAL aspect of the Act is not exempt from this approach: section 41 makes provision for 'Rules of Court' to be made concerning the appointment and duties of the GAL, and it also enables regulations to be made regarding the panels from which the GAL will be drawn. To be fair, this is more or less the approach which the existing legislation takes. As always, though, its disadvantage is the initial lack of certainty as to what is going to appear in the rules when they are eventually made. Two matters of concern, both to be regulated in this way, were given particular attention during the passage of the Act: the appointment of a solicitor to act alongside the guardian, and the independence of the guardian vis-a-vis the local authority.

With regard to solicitors, the generally accepted view is that the participation of experienced lawyers as representatives of children in care proceedings has been very beneficial. Whether appointed by the court, by the child's GAL, or by the child himself, they have been able to convey directly to the court the wishes of the child; a matter of particular importance in cases where they do not coincide with the GAL's views of what is in the child's interests. When the Children Bill was published, there were fears that these arrangements were to be curtailed. The Government indicated, however, that the Rules of Court would ensure the preservation of the present situation by authorising the GAL to instruct a solicitor to act on behalf of the child. Section 41 itself contains express provisions enabling the court to appoint a lawyer (it was these provisions which gave rise to the critics' fears): this can be done if for some reason no GAL has been appointed, or if the child has sufficient understanding and expresses a wish to instruct a solicitor, or if it appears to the court that legal representation would be in the child's best interests. The result, therefore, is that in 'specified proceedings' a solicitor may be drawn in to act for the child either on the initiative of the court, or on the initiative of the GAL (if one is appointed), or on the initiative of the child himself.

The independence of GALs is a much more contentious issue. The links between the existing GAL panels and the local authorities whose actions and proposals are, after all, the central reason for the appointment of guardians, have generated considerable anxiety. The essential point, and it is one that was fully recognised as soon as the existing legislation was passed in 1975, is that it is a contradiction in terms for provision to be made for independent second social work opinions in proceedings brought by a local authority, while at the same time having those second opinions delivered by social workers who are either employed by a local authority or organised and funded by a local authority. One solution to this problem is to establish a national GAL service, and proposals along these lines were made to the Government during the passage of the new Act. The response of the DoH was to urge the maintenance of the present framework pending the review of court welfare services generally (see below). Consequently, section 41 merely repeats the existing law by stating that the Secretary of State 'may by regulations provide for the establishment of panels of persons from whom guardians ad litem appointed under this section must be selected'.

This is not to say, however, that no changes are to be made in the administration of the GAL service. The Government indicated that it would use its regulation-making power to require the establishment of regional or sub-regional panels. These, it is argued, will be distanced from the local authorities which they serve. 'In some areas', it said, 'local authorities have already grouped themselves into consortia to operate joint arrangements. We would not wish to disturb any arrangements which are working well.' In addition, the appointment of panel managers will be provided for, and one of their more important tasks will be to monitor the work of the guardians and to oversee training and support programmes.

No doubt some improvement in the management of the GAL service will come about as a result of these new regulations. It is doubtful, however, whether the establishment of local authority consortia will be enough to meet the widespread concern which has been voiced about guardians' independence (not least by guardians themselves). One gets the impression that this is a view held by many within the DoH itself.

The content and delivery of the GAL's report

As with welfare reports under section 7, these matters will be largely regulated by the Rules of Court. Two matters are covered by the Act, though. The first is the relationship between the contents of the report and the strict rules of evidence and on this, section 41 contains a provision identical to the one in section 7 (noted earlier). The second concerns GALs' access to social services files. In order to put the matter beyond doubt, section 42 authorises a GAL to examine and take copies of all relevant material relating to the child held by a local authority (this does not mean just the authority involved in the GAL's case). Any such material which is copied will be admissible as evidence in the proceedings. The Government emphasised that the GAL will have free access to all material, not just the material on which the local authority intends to rely in court. Access to NSPCC and other non-SSD files will apparently be regulated by the Rules of Court.

Beyond the Children Act

In contrast to many of the other parts of the Act, the provisions concerning welfare reports and guardians ad litem are not the Government's last words. When the Act was introduced into Parliament, it was announced that the Government was putting in hand 'a programme of work which will extend step by step to all aspects of family law and business'. Included in this programme would be the organisation and function of welfare services (including the Official Solicitor). It was for this reason that proposals to incorporate in the Act provisions for a national GAL service were rejected: such proposals were, it was said, not necessarily undesirable, but simply premature. It may therefore be the case that the rules described in this chapter are mere stepping stones to a much more radical set-up whereby independent social workers (and lawyers) are appointed to safeguard the interests of children caught up in public and private law proceedings. Significantly, perhaps, the Minister of Health told the House of Commons that 'we may require completely different arrangements'. Plans for these are not likely to be published for some time.

15 The Children
and wardship

Introduction

The existence and modern development of the High Court's wardship jurisdiction has made life difficult for those seeking a full understanding of English child law, because it has always added an extra dimension to the legislative activity which has taken place. The boundaries of wardship have been fixed for the most part by the judges and the unhappy result has been that we have seen development of the law along two distinct channels: one in Parliament (legislation) and one in the courts (wardship). The benefits of wardship are well known: the case is handled by a professional judge and its outcome will be dictated, not by the application of rigid statutory criteria, but simply by what is in the child's best interests. In addition, the range of orders available to the judge is virtually limitless. During the 1970s and 1980s, local authorities, urged on by the judges, became increasingly aware of these attractive features and it is hardly surprising that many of them turned to wardship in preference to the widely criticised care jurisdiction of the juvenile courts. This attitude is encapsulated in the following comment made during the Children Act debates by an MP who was formerly a local authority solicitor:

> whenever I had the opportunity to do so, I would advise the local authority to make a child a ward instead of going to a juvenile court to obtain a care order. I felt satisfied with the standard of justice provided in the High Court and had confidence in the ability of a High Court judge, practising in the Family Division, to understand the nature of the case before him or her. Therefore, I seized every opportunity to take those cases to wardship.

Others seized every opportunity too, so that by 1985 local

.uthorities were thought to be involved in 40 per cent of wardship cases, as opposed to the 1971 figure of 3 per cent.

The principal object of the Children Act is to replace the numerous and chaotic statutory jurisdictions concerning children with a coherent and properly integrated framework, both in the 'private' and the 'public' spheres. Whether that object has been achieved will no doubt occasion debate, but nobody could reasonably dispute the comprehensive character of the Act. In these circumstances, the question inevitably arises: what should be done with wardship? One answer would be to abolish it completely, so that the only children's applications which could be made to the courts would be the ones set out in the Act. Parliament, following the advice of the Law Commission, has not gone this far. The argument seems to be that, while the Act does indeed bring in a completely new set of procedures and orders, not every contingency may have been foreseen. Wardship (or 'the High Court's inherent jurisdiction' as the Act calls it) should therefore be retained for those exceptional cases which slip through the statutory net.

However, what the Act has done is to impose restrictions on the use of wardship by or in favour of local authorities (as opposed to private individuals). This has been done because the Government believes that the new 'public' law framework concerning care and supervision orders is sufficiently comprehensive to be able to do without wardship in that particular area and that in any event State intervention should be strictly controlled by express statutory provisions. These restrictions are contained in section 100 of the Act, and although the wording of the section is open to different interpretations, its overall thrust is clear: where a statutory procedure is available to a local authority, that procedure, rather than wardship, must be used.

The effect of section 100: how local authorities are restricted

The restrictions are twofold. The first is that in future the courts will not be able to use wardship to place a child in local authority care, or to put a child under local authority supervision, or to confer on any local authority the power to decide any issue concerning an aspect of parental responsibility for a child. What this means is that if a local authority wishes to take over or retain the care of a child, or wants a supervision order, or wishes to assume some aspect of parental authority, it will be obliged to use the compulsory intervention procedures established by Parts IV and V of the Act (described in Chapters 7 to 11). This will, of course, involve the local authority in proving grounds for an order: no longer will it be

sufficient to argue simply on the basis of the welfare of t
Furthermore, if a care order is made, the local authority will
general control of the management of the case in accordan
the provisions of Part IV. The wardship court's existing po
give directions will simply not arise. The Act reinforces this po... by
stating that no care order child may be made a ward of court.

The second restriction is that in any event a local authority will be
unable to commence wardship proceedings without the leave of the
court. Leave may only be granted if the court is satisfied that there is
no statutory procedure available to the authority to achieve its
objective and that there is reasonable cause to believe that if the
wardship jurisdiction is not exercised the child concerned is likely to
suffer significant harm. This restriction keeps the door slightly ajar
for local authority wardship cases but stringent conditions are
imposed. The harm criterion harks back to Part IV of the Act and
reflects the need to control State intervention. Applications for care
orders and supervision orders will obviously not fall within this gap,
because of the first restriction noted above. Nor will orders which
give the local authority power to decide some issue of parental
responsibility, for the same reason. What, then, is left? There is in
fact no fixed list of situations in which local authorities will remain
free to use wardship (subject to leave); indeed, the open-ended
nature of the wardship jurisdiction precludes this.

During the Parliamentary debates, however, the Government
offered a few examples of cases which it thought might fall within
section 100; one of these was the case where a local authority looking
after a child wishes to obtain an injunction against some third party
prohibiting molestation etc. Other examples will be thrown up by
practical experience. In every case, it will be necessary to scan the
statute book to see if there is a procedure in existence which fits the
circumstances. If not, then wardship might be available. The scope
of section 100 is clearly one of the more complicated legal matters
arising under the Children Act and child care workers would do well
to seek legal advice at an early stage in situations where its
provisions may apply.

Wardship in the local authority context has attracted a large
number of devotees in recent years and it is therefore not surprising
that section 100 has been criticised by some commentators and
organisations as being unduly restrictive. Its logic, however, is
impeccable. If we go to the trouble of reviewing and then completely
recasting child law so as to get a comprehensive statutory package, it
makes no sense, and produces untold confusion, to permit applicants to circumvent the new framework by recourse to wardship.
Wardship is an anomalous and ancient jurisdiction whose limits are
unclear and which was never designed for the purposes to which it is
now put. If the compulsory intervention provisions of the Children

Act had been on the statute book twenty years ago, it is most unlikely that wardship would have been used so extensively by local authorities. Those who favour the procedure because of its High Court connections (the 'Rolls Royce factor') may find consolation in the fact that care proceedings will in future be able to be heard in that court (and it should be noted that if a magistrates' court refuses to transfer a care case upwards, the local authority will have an opportunity to appeal against the refusal).

What section 100 does not do is restrict the use of wardship by individuals (e.g. in disputes between parents or relatives). Logically, the argument used in relation to local authorities should apply here too, but the Government evidently felt that restrictions were unnecessary. In view of the new and wide range of section 8 orders (see Chapters 3 and 4), the number of 'private' wardship applications may be expected to decrease after the implementation of the Act. If, in such applications, the wardship court feels that local authority involvement may be needed, it can direct the authority to undertake an investigation (under section 37, discussed in Chapter 10). As we have seen, however, it is ultimately for the authority to decide whether or not to intervene: the court has no power of compulsion.

16 Voluntary homes and care in the private sector

Anyone casting an eye across the Children Act will notice that a substantial proportion of it is concerned with care outside the local authority sector. To be specific, there are sections or groups of sections (together with supplementary schedules) covering the following matters:

1 Voluntary homes (Part VII).
2 Private children's homes (Part VIII).
3 Private fostering (Part IX).
4 Child minding and day care for the under-eights (Part X).
5 Independent boarding schools (section 87).

These provisions will supersede the existing rules contained in the Nurseries and Child-Minders Regulation Act 1948, the Foster Children Act 1980, the Child Care Act 1980 and the Children's Homes Act 1982.

It is not proposed to analyse here the new rules concerning these subjects. This is partly due to reasons of space and partly because many of the provisions are technical and uncontroversial and to an extent a repeat performance of the existing law. Obviously those whose responsibilities lie in these areas will need to master the detail. What can be said about the provisions by way of general commentary, however, is that a number of themes clearly bind them together. We will find in most, though not all, of the sections covering the above topics, rules relating to:

1 Relevant definitions (e.g. 'voluntary home', 'privately fostered child', 'child minder').

2   The requirement to register or notify.

3   The power of the registering authority to impose requirements.

4   The cancellation of registration or the imposition of a prohibition.

5   The local authority's duty to satisfy itself that the child's welfare is being satisfactorily safeguarded and promoted.

6   The local authority's power to enter and inspect the premises.

7   Restrictions on who may be involved in the care of children.

8   The criminal liability of those who fail to register, breach requirements or prohibitions, or obstruct inspections.

9   Appeals against adverse decisions.

In every case, we find that the rules in the Act are to be supplemented by government regulations. These are certain to have a big impact on practice.

Although local authority involvement in these areas is to a large extent of a regulatory nature, two provisions in the Act require the authority to go further. The first is section 19. This imposes a duty on every authority to review periodically child minding and day care provision for the under-eights in its area. This complements the authority's duty to review its own day care facilities provided under section 18. The details of this are set out in Chapter 5. No doubt the results of the private sector review will affect the view the authority takes of its own provision (it may be noted at this point that section 18 expressly authorises an authority to provide advice and training facilities for those engaged in day care).

The second provision is section 24, which is concerned with after-care. The contents of this section are discussed in Chapter 6 from the perspective of children accommodated by local authorities. The important point for present purposes, however, is that the 'target group' also comprises those people under 21 who after the age of 16 spent time in voluntary sector accommodation, in a private children's home, or in a private foster home. The local authority's function of advising, befriending etc. extends to members of these groups, although there is a duty (as opposed to a discretion) only in relation to those leaving voluntary accommodation. Furthermore, an extra condition is inserted to the effect that the authority must be satisfied that the person or organisation which provided the accommodation does not have the necessary facilities for advising or befriending. To facilitate the provision of after-care, there is an obligation on the part of voluntary organisations and private homes to inform the local authority when a child over 16 leaves their care (this will be the authority within whose area the child proposes to live).

Foster care

In Chapter 19 there are noted the provisions of Schedule 7 of the Act regarding the number of children who can be fostered by any one person. These apply not only to local authority foster parents but also to foster parents working for voluntary organisations and private foster parents. The effect of exceeding the limit of three without an exemption from the local authority will be that the foster parent will be deemed to be carrying on a children's home. This will bring another set of statutory provisions into play. The Schedule provides for the establishment of complaints procedures relating to the way local authorities discharge their exemption functions.

17   Adoption

Introduction

One of the most welcome features of the Children Act is its 'fresh start' approach, whereby all of the basic rules concerning statutory children's procedures are set out in a self-contained package. Unhappily, this approach has not extended to the adoption procedure. Here, the Act does not set out the basic rules, these remain as stated in the Adoption Act 1976, but it proceeds, in Schedule 10, to introduce a number of amendments to these rules. In addition, some parts of the 1976 Act are repealed (by Schedule 15). The result is a rather unintelligible mish-mash of provisions. To be fair, this was probably unavoidable. The Children Act is not designed to reform adoption law; after all, comprehensive change was achieved in 1975, following the Houghton Committee review. But amendments to it were inevitable if the custody and care jurisdictions were to be altered, due to the various links between them. Having said this, some of the amendments have been inserted, not through necessity, but in order to correct deficiencies in the 1976 Act detected by the Department of Health in recent years.

For the moment, then, those working in the adoption field will need to be familiar with the 1976 Act (only fully implemented in 1988, of course) together with the amendments made by the Children Act. In the longer term, it looks as though we shall see a completely new Adoption Act, because the Government has announced that the whole area is to be the subject of a full-scale review.

The amendments made by Schedule 10

Some of the amendments made by Schedule 10 are purely technical and will have little significance in practice. Those worthy of note are as follows:

● The formal effect of an adoption order is now to vest 'parental responsibility' for the child in the adopters, as opposed to 'the parental rights and duties'. As we saw in Chapter 2, the latter expression is being dropped from children's legislation.

● An adoption order will extinguish the parental responsibility which anybody had before it; the order will also extinguish any order previously made under the Children Act (whether of a 'private' or 'public' nature).

● The normal minimum age limit for married applicants remains at 21. However, where one of the applicants is a natural parent of the child, the limit for that parent is now 18.

● The statutory ground for dispensing with parental agreement due to persistent failure to discharge the parental duties now refers to a persistent failure to discharge parental responsibility.

● Under section 18 of the Adoption Act, an application to free a child for adoption may be made where the agency is applying for dispensation of the natural parents' agreement and the child 'is in the care of' the agency. Schedule 10 restricts this procedure to local authorities which hold a care order in respect of the child. This type of freeing application will consequently cease to be available in cases where the child is being looked after on a voluntary basis. Here we have yet another illustration of the way in which the Children Act confines compulsory State intervention to the care order jurisdiction. It should be noted, however, that if one of the parents consents, a freeing application can be made in respect of an 'accommodated' child.

● A freeing order will, of course, now vest parental responsibility in the agency, instead of 'the parental rights and duties'.

● Section 22 of the Adoption Act requires a minimum of three months notice to be given to the local authority in the case of a non-agency application for adoption. In order to deal with stale cases, Schedule 10 now introduces a maximum period of notice: such an application shall not be made unless the person wishing to make the application has, within the period of two years preceding the making of the application, given notice. This links in with an amendment which has been made to the definition of a 'protected child', for such a status will in future cease two years after the giving of a section 22 notice if no adoption application has been made. The significance of this for social services departments is that no further welfare supervision need be undertaken; indeed, the case can be regarded as closed.

● Birth records counselling, mandatory, of course, for those adopted before 12 November 1975, may now be provided by organisations other than those (British-based ones) mentioned in section 51 of the Adoption Act if the applicant is not living in the UK.

● An Adoption Contact Register is to be set up and maintained by the Registrar General. This will be a computerised service designed to assist those adopted persons and their natural relatives (i.e. persons who are related by blood, including half-blood, or marriage) who desire to establish contact with each other. The Register will be in two parts, Part I for adopted persons and Part II for relatives. Anybody within these categories who is over 18 and possesses a sufficient amount of relevant information will, on payment of a fee, be able to enter himself or herself on the appropriate part. Once an adopted person and a relative of his appear on the Register, the Registrar General will transmit the latter's name and address to the former. The address may not be the relative's own address. As the Minister of Health explained:

> Many relatives will no doubt be happy to give their own address, but care and sensitivity are needed where people are seeking knowledge of each other in these often delicate circumstances. Some people prefer to make a first approach through an intermediary with skill and experience in smoothing the path for both parties. These arrangements will also allow relatives to explain through a sympathetic intermediary that they prefer to restrict contact to, say, the exchange of information or letters, rather than a meeting. Some voluntary agencies have already expressed a willingness to provide their addresses and services.

Actually making contact is, of course, left to the two parties, although the Government has stated that as part of the administration of the scheme, the Registrar General will inform those using it of the advice and assistance available from agencies.

● The experimental arrangements for the payment by agencies of adoption allowances are retained, although the legal framework will in future be different. Instead of the DoH having to approve individual agency schemes, country-wide regulations will be made authorising all agencies to make payments. These regulations will inevitably be fairly detailed, covering such matters as agency procedure, criteria for eligibility and quantification of payments. This change seems a sensible one, in view of the widespread use of allowances since their introduction in 1982 (thoroughly documented in Lambert and Seglow, *Adoption Allowances in England and Wales: The Early Years* (1988) HMSO). The Government's expressed intention is to 'give agencies sufficient flexibility to respond to a diversity of circumstances'.

The repeals effected by Schedule 15

Schedule 15 does away with a number of provisions of the 1976 Act:

● The existing power of the court, given by section 26 of the 1976 Act, to order a committal to care or local authority supervision on the refusal of an adoption application, is removed. In future, an adoption court will, if it desires local authority intervention, use section 37 of the Children Act to direct an investigation by the authority (see Chapter 10). Alternatively, the court could make a family assistance order under section 16 (on which see Chapter 3). Since adoption proceedings are classed by the Act as 'family proceedings', it is also open to the court to make a section 8 order. So, for example, the court will have the power to refuse an adoption order but grant a residence order and a contact order instead.

● Following on from the final point made in the previous paragraph, the provisions in the 1976 Act which are designed to discourage step-parent adoptions following the natural parents' divorce (sections 14(3) and 15(4)) are repealed. These have always been difficult provisions in the sense that their wording is less than satisfactory, leading different courts to adopt different approaches. The policy behind them has also been controversial. Their disappearance, of course, will not mean an end to the controversy. In future, where a step-parent or a relative (or anybody else, for that matter) applies to adopt, although custody or custodianship will not be available as an alternative (since the Children Act abolishes them), a residence order will be. Such an order, like custody, is not as drastic in its legal effect as adoption. In many cases, therefore, social workers and judges will continue to have to make difficult judgements about the respective merits of the two types of order.

● The power of the juvenile court to make a place of safety order in respect of a protected child (section 34) is removed and replaced by the emergency protection powers created by Part V of the Children Act.

18 Young offenders

The Children Act is not designed to be a vehicle for radical and comprehensive reform of the law relating to young offenders. Its emphasis is very firmly on the non-criminal side. Nevertheless, some mention of the criminal jurisdiction was always going to be necessary, simply because a care order is one of the disposals currently available to the juvenile court after a conviction: section 7(7)(a) of the Children and Young Persons Act 1969 enables a care order to be made if the offence is punishable in the case of an adult with imprisonment. As care orders within the meaning of the 1969 Act are abolished by the 1989 Act, the provisions of section 7(7)(a) need replacing.

The solution seized upon by the Government is to expand the concept of the criminal supervision order so that it can embrace a requirement that the offender reside in local authority accommodation. In this way, many of the existing features of criminal care orders can be retained but they will appear in a legal framework which does not confuse those children convicted of offences and those in need of protection. To emphasise this bifurcation of the care and criminal jurisdictions, the Children Act, while recasting the former in Part IV, ensures that the latter remains governed by the 1969 Act. The 'criminal' bits and pieces of the 1969 Act therefore stay on the statute book (the same point is encountered in relation to supervision orders, see Chapter 11).

The relevant amendments to the 1969 Act are set out in Schedule 12 of the Children Act. According to these, the court may include in a supervision order a requirement that the child or young person lives for a specified period in accommodation provided by or on behalf of the local authority in whose area he is resident. The order may provide that the child shall not live with a named person. The maximum period which may be specified, however, is six months. This can, of course, be contrasted with the indeterminate length of the criminal care order made under the existing provisions.

The new type of requirement just described is referred to in the Act as a 'residence requirement'. Before it can be imposed, a number of conditions must be satisfied. These are as follows:

1 A supervision order has previously been made in respect of the child or young person.
2 That order imposed a requirement under section 12A(3) of the 1969 Act (this refers to intermediate treatment etc. directed by the court) or a residence requirement.
3 The offence was committed while that order was in force.
4 The offence is punishable with imprisonment if committed by a person over 21.
5 The offence is in the court's opinion a serious one.
6 The court is satisfied that the behaviour which constituted the offence was due, to a significant extent, to the circumstances in which the child was living (this condition does not apply in a case where a residence requirement is already in existence).
7 The relevant local authority has been consulted.

These conditions make it clear that the making of a supervision order with a residence requirement is only appropriate, and, indeed, only available in the case of a child who, in the Government's words, 'has a history of offending and who has already been required to participate in community-based activities'. Careful note should also be taken of the sixth condition, concerning the home circumstances of the child. This condition is related to the very nature of the residence requirement, namely that the child is to be removed to local authority accommodation. The Government's thinking is that the social services department will, for the duration of the requirement, work with the child's family 'in the hope that the home circumstances leading to his offending behaviour will be ameliorated'. The fifth condition, concerning the gravity of the offence, is designed to remind magistrates that a residence requirement, which can and will be viewed by some as a custodial sentence, is not to be imposed lightly.

Remands to local authority accommodation

Another change made necessary by the new care provisions is the rewriting of section 23 of the 1969 Act, which deals with the remand of young defendants charged with criminal offences. Schedule 12 substitutes a new version of section 23 which in substance is very similar to the existing one, except that instead of the court committing the child to the care of the local authority, it will now 'remand him to local authority accommodation'. Such a remand will not entail any transfer of parental rights to the authority (as will a care order) but the authority will be in a position to do whatever is reasonable for the purpose of safeguarding or promoting the child's welfare: this stems from section 3(5) of the Act which, as we have seen in earlier chapters, is one of its provisions of general application. In addition, the child will fall into the category of those being 'looked after' by the authority and hence the code of treatment, described in Chapter 6, will apply (except for the parental contribution rules).

Recovery of absentees

Section 32 of the 1969 Act is rewritten by Schedule 12 so as to authorise the police to arrest anywhere in the UK or the Channel Islands a child who is absent without leave from local authority accommodation to which he has been removed under a residence requirement or a remand.

The need for a consolidating measure

These changes in the law relating to young offenders are the latest in a series of moves which the present Government has made in this field. Practitioners in the area will already be familiar with the amendments introduced by the Criminal Justice Acts of 1982 and 1988. Leaving aside the various policy arguments which can be made in respect of these changes, it must be obvious by now that the legislation is in urgent need of restatement. It is to be hoped that a consolidating statute will emerge in the near future so that the rules become more accessible.

19 Local authority foster parents

The expression 'local authority foster parent' is a new arrival on the statute book. Section 23 of the Children Act defines such a person as anyone with whom a child being 'looked after' by a local authority has been placed, unless he is a parent of the child, a non-parent with parental responsibility, or, in the case of a care order child, a person who held a residence order prior to the care order being made.

Reference has been made in earlier chapters to provisions of the Act which specifically refer to local authority foster parents. To summarise, these are the provisions governing applications for section 8 orders (Chapter 4), DoH regulations on foster placements (Chapter 6) and local authority complaints procedures (also Chapter 6). There are, however, two further provisions worthy of note.

Foster parent recruitment

According to Schedule 2, every local authority shall, in making any arrangements designed to encourage persons to act as local authority foster parents, 'have regard to the different racial groups to which children within their area who are in need belong'. This obligation owes its existence to pressure exerted by the Commission for Racial Equality, which has expressed concern about the lack of progress being made by some social services departments in recruiting foster parents from ethnic minority groups. It complements the requirement contained in section 22 of the Act under which an authority, in making any decision with respect to a child, is to give due consideration to his religious persuasion, racial origin and cultural and linguistic background (on which see page 61).

A careful reading of these provisions shows that they do not require SSDs to follow a strong policy of same-race placements. They were certainly not intended to have this effect. On the other hand, they are consistent with the view that such placements have much to offer, and they can therefore be expected to be seized upon with alacrity by authorities with a particularly vigorous commitment to equal opportunities. One of their obvious implications lies in the field of staffing. If authorities are to cater for black children effectively, e.g. by the recruitment of more black foster parents, then the number of black social workers may need to be increased.

Limit on number of children

The second provision is Schedule 7. This is designed to limit the number of children a foster parent looks after. It covers not just local authority foster parents but also foster parents working for voluntary organisations and private foster parents; indeed, it appears to have been inspired partly by problems of overcrowding in the private sector. Schedule 7 states that a person may not foster more than three children. There is, however, plenty of room for exceptions. In the first place, the limit can be exceeded if the children concerned are all siblings. Secondly, foster parents can be given permission to exceed the limit by the authority in whose area they live. Thirdly, government regulations can (and presumably will) be made authorising a breach of the limit in cases of urgency. The result is that, for local authority foster parents, the three children limit is more of a guideline than a rule.

20 Transitional and other provisions of the Act

Not every section and subsection of the Children Act has been described in this book. The approach has been a selective one, based on a consideration of the needs of the likely readership. In this final chapter, I propose to describe a number of provisions which could not be conveniently dovetailed into the previous ones but which are sufficiently important to justify a mention.

The transitional provisions

It will be apparent from everything that has gone before that the effect of the Act on the work of the social services will be nothing short of revolutionary. This effect will be felt most keenly on implementation day when practices and terminology will have to change. An important group of children will be caught by this revolution: those who are already the subject of court or local authority intervention. How will their position be affected? The answers to this vital question lie in Schedule 14 of the Act, which bears the innocuous title 'Transitionals and Savings'.

Schedule 14 is necessarily very long and complicated because it aims to set out the legal position of all those children who are in 'the system' or who have been through it. Its more important features are now summarised:

● Court proceedings which are pending on implementation day will, as a rule, proceed under the 'old law'.

● A person holding a custody or custodianship order made under the old law will, on implementation day, have parental responsibility for the child if he or she does not already have it.

● References in the Act to holders of residence orders will cover holders of custody and custodianship orders made under the old law.

● References in the Act to holders of contact orders will cover holders of access orders made under the old law.

● A residence order or a care order made under the Act will have the effect of discharging a custody, custodianship or access order made under the old law.

● It will be possible to apply to the court for discharge of any custody, custodianship or access order made under the old law.

● Children who are the subject of a care order made under section 1 of the Children and Young Persons Act 1969, children who are the subject of a parental rights resolution and children who have been committed to care in family proceedings, will all be deemed to be subject to a care order made under the Children Act. This means, of course, that the code of treatment, the new contact provisions and the other supplementary rules will apply to them. Any access order made under the Child Care Act 1980 will be treated as a new-style contact order.

● Children in voluntary care will be deemed to be in section 20 accommodation. The 28 day notice rule will consequently cease to apply and the parents will have the right to remove the child at any time.

● The after-care provisions in section 24 will apply to those under-21s who will have been in local authority care under the old law.

● Supervision orders made in care proceedings under the Children and Young Persons Act 1969 will be treated as supervision orders made under the 1989 Act. Their duration may be affected by this. Supervision orders made in family proceedings will not be treated in this way. They will continue in force, but only for a year beyond implementation day.

● Criminal care orders made under the 1969 Act will continue in force but only for six months beyond implementation day (unless discharged earlier). This rule reflects the new arrangements made for dealing with young offenders (described in Chapter 18).

Refuges for children at risk

Section 51 of the Act contains long-awaited provisions regulating

refuges for runaway children. The voluntary sector is very act
this field, especially the Children's Society, and there has .
anxiety in recent years about the legal status of safe houses; then
after all, a fairly elaborate body of legislation relating to the
abduction and harbouring of children. The DoH always intended
the reform of child law to take in the question of refuges and the end
product is section 51. For a description of the effect of this section,
we may take the words of the Minister of Health when addressing
the House of Commons:

> organisations and persons providing refuges may be issued with a
> certificate by the Secretary of State and where a certificate is in force,
> those running the refuge, whether in children's homes or as foster
> parents, cannot be prosecuted for offences involving, for example,
> harbouring. Regulations will impose rigorous requirements on those
> running refuges.

Children accommodated in hospitals, nursing homes and schools

In its 1987 White Paper, the DoH expressed concern about the
welfare of children who are accommodated for long spells in
hospitals or nursing homes and children who are placed in
residential schools by education departments. There is evidence that
significant numbers of these children lose contact with their families.
To meet this concern, sections 85 and 86 of the Act require the
relevant SSD to be notified of the child's situation by any health
authority, education department, residential care home, nursing
home or mental nursing home which is providing him with
accommodation for a consecutive period of three months or more.
Upon notification, the SSD must take such steps as are reasonably
practicable to enable it to determine whether the child's welfare is
being adequately safeguarded and promoted. It must also consider
whether it should exercise any of its functions under the Act (e.g.
support functions under Part III).

When the child leaves such accommodation, the SSD must be
informed. If the child is over 16, he becomes 'a person qualifying for
advice and assistance' for the purposes of the after-care provisions
of the Act (on which see Chapter 6). The accommodating authority
or home must accordingly inform the SSD within whose area the
child proposes to live.

The effect of the sections will be to impose additional burdens on
SSDs. The extent of these, in terms of the number of children
involved, remains unclear, however.

Index